Microsoft® Office Excel 2003

Level 1

Vincent Iglesias-Cardinale

Microsoft® Office Excel 2003: Level 1

Part Number: 084260
Course Edition: 1.11

ACKNOWLEDGMENTS

Project Team

Curriculum Developer and Technical Writer: Vincent Iglesias-Cardinale • **Content Manager:** Chris Clark • **Content Editors:** J-P Altieri, Margaux Phillips and Laura Thomas • **Material Editor:** Elizabeth M. Swank • **Graphic Designer:** Larry Conrow • **Project Technical Specialist:** Michael Toscano

NOTICES

HELP US IMPROVE OUR COURSEWARE

Your comments are important to us. Please contact us at Element K Press LLC, 1-800-478-7788, 500 Canal View Boulevard, Rochester, NY 14623, Attention: Product Planning, or through our Web site at **http://support.elementkcourseware.com.**

NOTES

MICROSOFT® OFFICE EXCEL 2003: LEVEL 1

Contents

Microsoft® Office Excel 2003: Level

Contents

ABOUT THIS COURSE

You have basic computer skills such as using a mouse, navigating through windows, and surfing the Internet. You have also used paper-based systems to store data that you run calculations on. You now want to migrate that data to an electronic format. In this course, you will use Microsoft® Office Excel 2003 to manage, edit, and print data.

Imagine you are using a paper-based method to store sales data (similar in kind to the spreadsheet in Figure 0-1). You need to add a new row of data for a new sales associate.

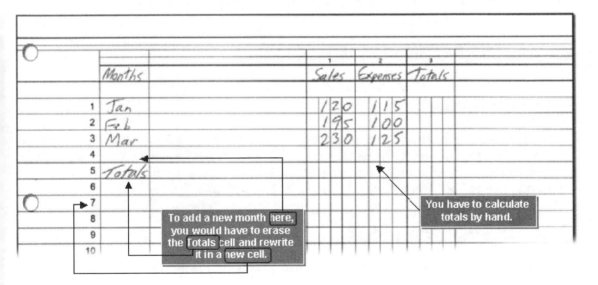

Figure 0-1: *A paper-based spreadsheet that stores sales data.*

Now, imagine storing that same data electronically in an Excel file, as illustrated in Figure 0-2.

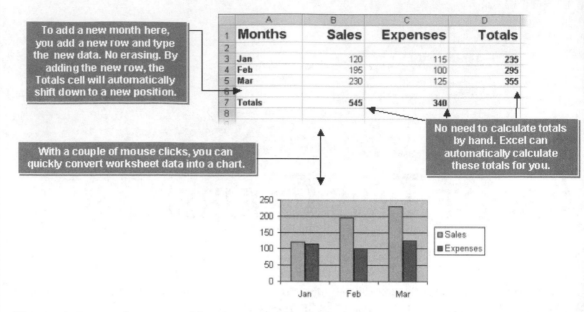

Figure 0-2: *An electronic file that stores sales data.*

Storing data electronically is more efficient because it allows you to quickly update existing data, run reports on the data, calculate totals, and chart, sort, and filter your data.

Course Description

Target Student

This course is designed for persons preparing for certification as a Microsoft® Office Specialist in Excel, who already have knowledge of the Microsoft® Office Windows 98 (or above) operating system, and who desire to gain the skills necessary to create, edit, format, and print basic Microsoft® Excel 2003 worksheets.

Course Prerequisites

To ensure your success, we recommend you first take the following Element K course or have equivalent knowledge:

*   *Microsoft Office Windows XP: Introduction*

If you have taken an introductory course for an earlier version of the Windows operating system, this will also meet the prerequisite.

How to Use This Book

As a Learning Guide

Each lesson covers one broad topic or set of related topics. Lessons are arranged in order of increasing proficiency with *Microsoft® Excel 2003*; skills you acquire in one lesson are used and developed in subsequent lessons. For this reason, you should work through the lessons in sequence.

We organized each lesson into results-oriented topics. Topics include all the relevant and supporting information you need to master *Microsoft® Excel 2003*, and activities allow you to apply this information to practical hands-on examples.

You get to try out each new skill on a specially prepared sample file. This saves you typing time and allows you to concentrate on the skill at hand. Through the use of sample files, hands-on activities, illustrations that give you feedback at crucial steps, and supporting background information, this book provides you with the foundation and structure to learn *Microsoft® Excel 2003* quickly and easily.

As a Review Tool

Any method of instruction is only as effective as the time and effort you are willing to invest in it. In addition, some of the information that you learn in class may not be important to you immediately, but it may become important later on. For this reason, we encourage you to spend some time reviewing the topics and activities after the course. For additional challenge when reviewing activities, try the "What You Do" column before looking at the "How You Do It" column.

As a Reference

The organization and layout of the book make it easy to use as a learning tool and as an after-class reference. You can use this book as a first source for definitions of terms, background information on given topics, and summaries of procedures.

This course is one of a series of Element K courseware titles that addresses Microsoft Office Specialist (Office Specialist) skill sets. The Office Specialist program is for individuals who use Microsoft's business desktop software and who seek recognition for their expertise with specific Microsoft products. Certification candidates must pass one or more proficiency exams in order to earn Office Specialist certification.

Course Objectives

In this course, you will create and edit basic Microsoft® Office Excel 2003 worksheets and workbooks.

You will:

- create a basic worksheet.
- modify a worksheet.
- perform calculations.
- format a worksheet.

- develop a workbook.
- print the contents of a workbook.
- customize the layout of the Excel window.

Course Requirements

Hardware

For this course, you will need one computer for each student and one for the instructor. Each computer will need the following minimum hardware components:

- A 233 MHz Pentium-class processor if you use Microsoft® Office Windows XP Professional as your operating system. 300 MHz is recommended.
- A 133 MHz Pentium-class processor if you use Microsoft® Office Windows 2000 Professional as your operating system.
- 128 MB of RAM.
- A 6 GB hard disk or larger.
- A floppy disk drive.
- A mouse or other pointing device.
- An 800 x 600 resolution monitor.
- Network cards and cabling for local network access.
- Internet access (see your local network administrator).
- A printer (optional).
- A projection system to display the instructor's computer screen.

Software

- Either Windows XP Professional with Service Pack 1, or Windows 2000 Professional with Service Pack 4.
- Microsoft® Office Professional Edition 2003.

Class Setup

For Initial Class Setup

1. Install Windows 2000 Professional or Windows XP Professional on an empty partition.
   - Leave the Administrator password blank.
   - For all other installation parameters, use values that are appropriate for your environment (see your local network administrator if you need details).
2. On Windows 2000 Professional, when the Network Identification Wizard runs after installation, select the option Users Must Enter A User Name And Password To Use This Computer. (This step ensures that students will be able to log on as the Administrator user regardless of what other user accounts exist on the computer.)

3. On Windows 2000 Professional, in the Getting Started With Windows 2000 window, uncheck Show This Screen At Startup. Click Exit.

4. On Windows 2000 Professional, set 800 x 600 display resolution: Right-click the desktop and choose Properties. Select the Settings tab. Move the Screen Area slider to 800 By 600 Pixels. Click OK twice, then click Yes.

5. On Windows 2000 Professional, install Service Pack 4. Use the Service Pack installation defaults.

6. On Windows XP Professional, disable the Welcome screen. (This step ensures that students will be able to log on as the Administrator user regardless of what other user accounts exist on the computer.) Click Start and choose Control Panel→User Accounts. Click Change The Way Users Log On And Off. Uncheck Use Welcome Screen. Click Apply Options.

7. On Windows XP Professional, install Service Pack 1. Use the Service Pack installation defaults.

8. On either operating system, install a printer driver (a physical print device is optional).

   — For Windows XP Professional, click Start and choose Printers And Faxes. Under Printer Tasks, click Add A Printer and follow the prompts.

   — For Windows 2000 Professional, click Start and choose Settings→Printers. Run the Add Printer Wizard and follow the prompts.

9. Run the Internet Connection Wizard to set up the Internet connection as appropriate for your environment, if you did not do so during installation.

10. Log on to the computer as the Administrator user if you have not already done so.

11. Perform a Complete installation of the Microsoft® Office System.

12. Minimize the Language Bar if it appears.

13. On the course CD-ROM, open the 084_260 folder. Then, open the Data folder. Run the 084260dd.exe self-extracting file located within. This will install a folder named 084260Data on your C drive. This folder contains all the data files that you will use to complete this course.

14. Move all folders from 084260Data to the My Documents folder for the Administrator user.

15. Create a desktop shortcut to the course data files folder. Rename the shortcut "Excel Level 1."

Before Every Class

1. Log on to the computer as the Administrator user.

2. Delete any existing data files from the My Documents folder.

3. Extract a fresh copy of the course data files from the CD-ROM provided with the course manual and move them to the My Documents folder for the Administrator user.

List of Additional Files

Printed with each activity is a list of files students open to complete that activity. Many activities also require additional files that students do not open, but are needed to support the file(s) students are working with. These supporting files are included with the student data files on the course CD-ROM or data disk. Do not delete these files.

NOTES

LESSON 1
Getting Started with Excel

Lesson Objectives:

In this lesson, you will create a basic worksheet.

You will:

*   Identify key components of the Excel environment.
*   Navigate through the Excel environment.
*   Select data.
*   Enter data.
*   Save a workbook.
*   Obtain help using Excel's Help system.

Introduction

You have heard that Microsoft® Office Excel 2003 can help you store and manage alphanumeric data. However, you are not yet familiar with the basic elements of Excel. In this lesson, you will be introduced to basic concepts that will help you get started using Excel.

You would never use a computer without first having a basic understanding of its components and how it operates. Figure 1-1 shows the basic components of a computer.

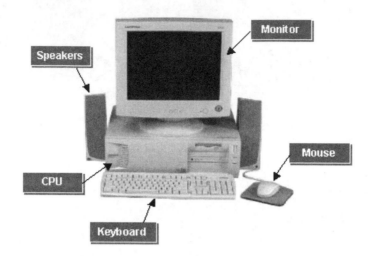

Figure 1-1: *Basic components of a computer*.

Understanding the basic components of Excel prior to using it will give you a familiarity with the application and make you a more efficient user.

TOPIC A

An Overview of Excel

You want to use Excel to store and manipulate data. You now need to begin familiarizing yourself with key components of the Excel environment so that you can recognize these components when necessary. In this topic, you will receive an overview of Excel and its core components.

Imagine you have just accepted a new job. On the first day of work, you walk in the door and your new manager says, "Welcome! Here's your cube. Get to work," and then disappears for the remainder of the day. Wouldn't it be easier for you to perform in your new job if you received an overview of how to work in your new environment? An overview of Excel will help familiarize you with some of Excel's basic concepts so that you won't be lost when you begin to fully deploy the application.

Spreadsheets

Definition:

A spreadsheet is a form used to store and manipulate numbers, text, and non-alphanumeric symbols. All spreadsheets consist of a grid of columns and rows that intersect to form cells. Cells store the data entered into a spreadsheet. Columns appear vertically and are identified by letters; rows appear horizontally and are identified by numbers.

Some spreadsheets are paper-based, others can be stored electronically.

Spreadsheets differ from one another based upon their associated business needs and data requirements.

Example: An Electronic Spreadsheet

The following figure, Figure 1-2, is an example of an electronic spreadsheet.

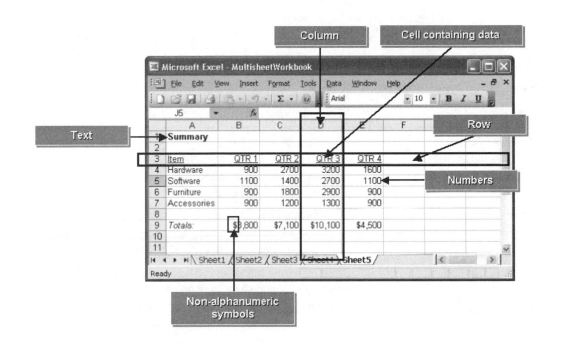

Figure 1-2: *An electronic spreadsheet.*

The Excel Application Window

When you open Excel, two windows are displayed, one within the other. The outer window is the main application window, and the inner window is the workbook window. The *application window* usually fills the entire screen and provides a place for you to interact with Excel. The *workbook window* appears within the application window and displays a workbook in which to enter and store data. Figure 1-3 shows some common components of the Excel environment.

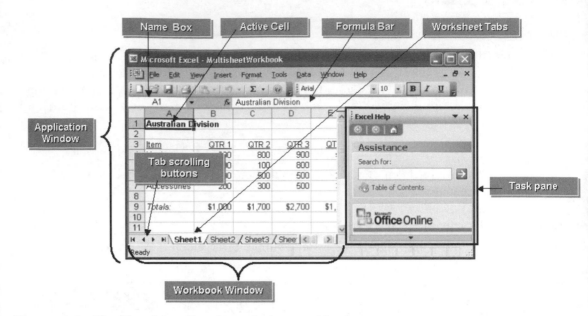

Figure 1-3: *The Excel application window and its key components.*

Table 1-1: *Excel Window Elements*

Window Element	Description
Formula bar	Appears below the toolbars and displays the contents of the active cell in a workbook.
Name Box	Appears above the column A heading and displays the name of the current or active cell.
Active cell	The currently selected cell.
Worksheet tabs	Appear at the bottom of the workbook and allow you to move from one worksheet to another.
Tab scrolling buttons	Appear to the left of the sheet tabs and allow you to scroll the display of the worksheet tabs one at a time, or display the first or last grouping of sheet tabs within a workbook.
Task pane	Appears to the right of the workbook window on an as-needed basis.

Worksheets and Workbooks

An Excel *worksheet* is an electronic spreadsheet. By default, Excel designates column headings with letters running across the top of the worksheet. Column headings begin with the letter A and continue through the letter Z. After the 26th column (column Z), headings become double letters, from AA to IV. Row headings are designated with numbers running down the left border of the worksheet. Row headings begin with the number 1 and continue through the number 65536, as shown in Figure 1-4.

An Excel *workbook* is a repository of related worksheets. The default Excel workbook contains three worksheets named Sheet1, Sheet2, and Sheet3. An Excel workbook file can contain up to 255 separate worksheets. The worksheet names appear on tabs at the bottom of the workbook, as shown in Figure 1-4.

When you open a new workbook, the cell that is selected is the *active cell.*

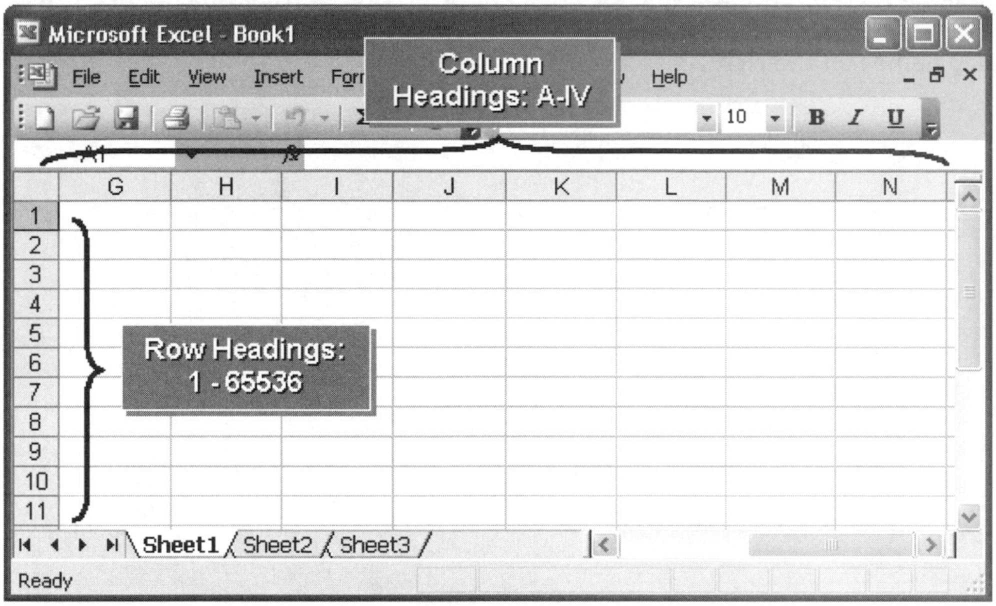

Figure 1-4: *Column and row headings.*

DISCOVERY ACTIVITY 1-1

Identifying Key Components of Spreadsheets and the Excel Environment

Objective:

To identify key components of spreadsheets and the Excel environment.

Scenario:

To get more comfortable with Excel, you will identify key components of spreadsheets and the Excel environment.

LESSON 1

1. Each graphic on the left has a specific component of a spreadsheet highlighted by a thick black box. Match the highlighted component in the graphics with their corresponding names on the right.

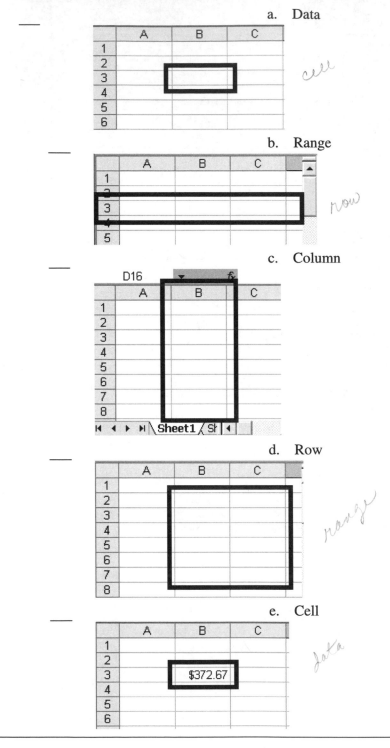

a. Data

cell

b. Range

row

c. Column

d. Row

range

e. Cell

data

2. Each graphic on the left has a specific component of the Excel environment highlighted by a thick black box. Match the highlighted component in the graphics with their corresponding names on the right.

_c_   a. Tab scrolling buttons

_i_   b. Formatting toolbar

_e_   c. Name Box

_j_   d. Formula Bar

_h_   e. Title bar

_a_   f. Standard toolbar

_f_   g. Task pane

_b_   h. Worksheet tabs

_g_   i. Active cell

_d_   j. Menu bar

TOPIC B

Navigate in Excel

You are familiar with the characteristics of spreadsheets and the components of the Excel environment. In this topic, you will navigate to those components.

Imagine you've just moved to a new city to start a new job. You've only been in the new place for about a week and haven't really had time to take a closer look at the city. You've set aside time on the upcoming weekend to drive around the city and begin familiarizing yourself with some of the landmarks. Learning the basics of navigating in Excel is much like the move to the new city: you know how to drive (click the mouse, open menus, and so on), but you don't know the terrain yet. By navigating around Excel, you begin to understand its terrain, thus making it easier for you to use the application.

How to Navigate in Excel

There are a number of ways to move around in Excel. To move to a specific cell or range of cells, you can use the mouse or the keyboard. The following tables describe how to use the mouse and keyboard to navigate in Excel (see Table 1-2 and Table 1-3).

Table 1-2: *Using the Mouse to Navigate in Excel*

To	Do this
Move the worksheet display up or down one row per click.	Click a vertical scroll arrow.
Move the worksheet display left or right one column per click.	Click a horizontal scroll arrow.
Continuously move the worksheet display horizontally or vertically.	Continuously click the mouse button while placing the mouse pointer inside the horizontal or vertical scroll arrow.
Move the worksheet display one screen at a time.	Click between the scroll box and the scroll arrow of either the horizontal or vertical scroll bar.
Move rapidly, either vertically or horizontally, through the worksheet area.	Drag the scroll boxes.
Move to the cell specified in the cell reference.	Click in the Name Box, type the cell reference, and press Enter.

Table 1-3: *Using the Keyboard*

To Move the Active Cell	Do this
One cell at a time to the left, right, up, or down.	Press the corresponding arrow keys.
To column A of the current row.	Press Home.
Down or up by one screen's worth of rows.	Press Page Down or Page Up.
To the right, one cell at a time.	Press Tab.
To the left, one cell at a time.	Press Shift+Tab.
To cell A1 in the active worksheet.	Press Ctrl+Home.

To Move the Active Cell	Do this
One screen to the left or right, respectively.	Press Alt+Page Up to go left. Press Alt+Page Down to go right.

ACTIVITY 1-2

Navigating in Excel

Objective:

To navigate in Excel.

Data Files:

- NavigationPractice

Scenario:

You have just returned to your office from a full day of Excel training, and, in an effort to reinforce your memory, you have just reviewed the key components of spreadsheets and the Excel environment. To help reinforce the basic concepts of navigating in Excel, the instructor also recommended that students practice navigating in the Excel environment as soon as possible after the course. You are now ready to practice navigating in Excel.

What You Do	How You Do It
1. Start Excel.	a. On the Windows taskbar, **click Start.**
	b. **Choose All Programs→Microsoft Office→ Microsoft Office Excel 2003.**
2. Open the NavigationPractice file, and then view the last record.	a. **Choose File→Open** to display the Open dialog box.
	b. **Click the Desktop icon** in the left pane of the Open dialog box.
	c. **Double-click the Excel Level 1 folder.**
	d. **Double-click the NavigationPractice file name.**

e. **Drag the vertical scroll bar down as far as it will go.**

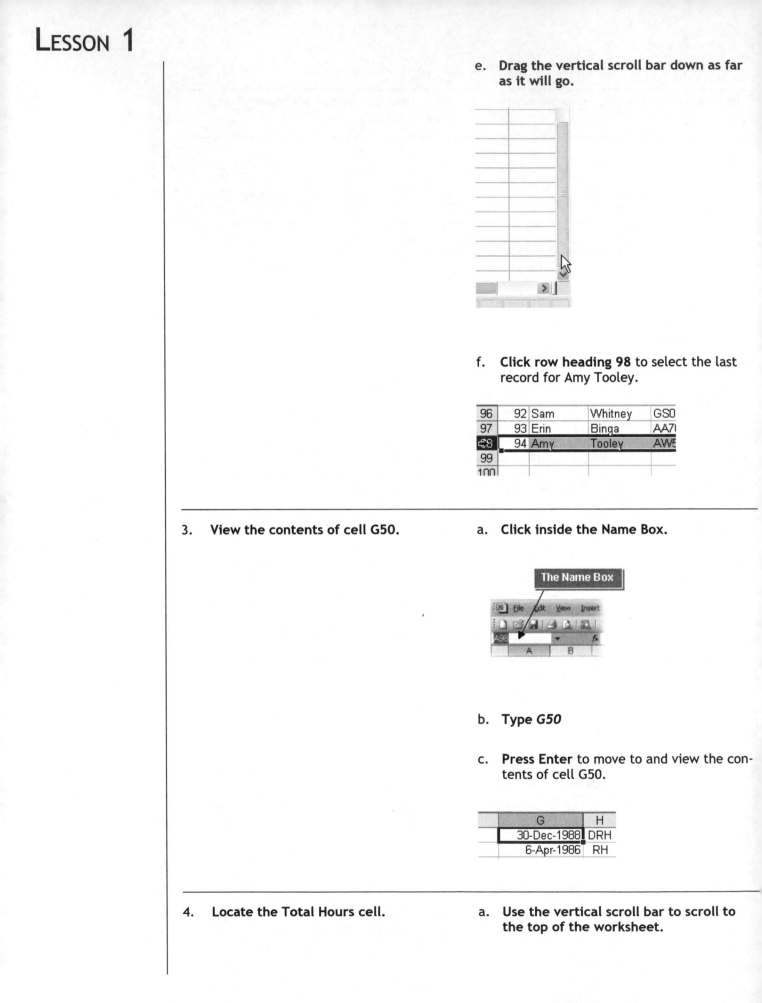

f. **Click row heading 98** to select the last record for Amy Tooley.

3. **View the contents of cell G50.**

a. **Click inside the Name Box.**

b. **Type** *G50*

c. **Press Enter** to move to and view the contents of cell G50.

4. **Locate the Total Hours cell.**

a. **Use the vertical scroll bar to scroll to the top of the worksheet.**

b. **Use the horizontal scroll bar to scroll to the right of the worksheet until you see the Total Hours cell.**

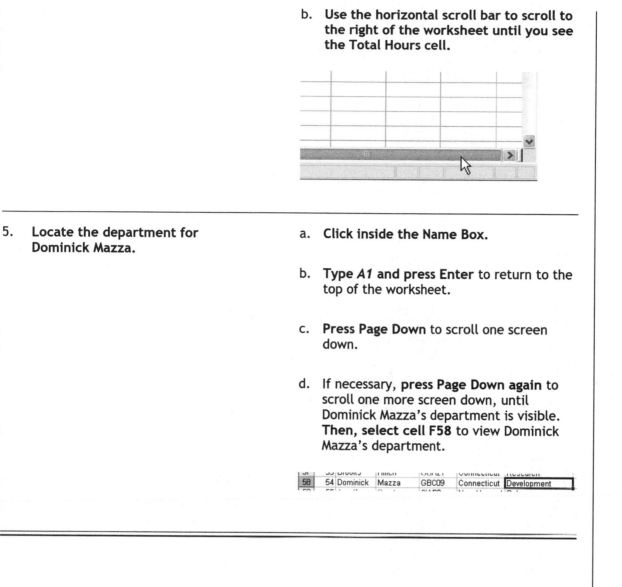

5. **Locate the department for Dominick Mazza.**

a. **Click inside the Name Box.**

b. **Type *A1* and press Enter** to return to the top of the worksheet.

c. **Press Page Down** to scroll one screen down.

d. If necessary, **press Page Down again** to scroll one more screen down, until Dominick Mazza's department is visible. **Then, select cell F58** to view Dominick Mazza's department.

TOPIC C

Select Data

You have familiarized yourself with the Excel environment. Now you're ready to work with data. One of the first things you need to do is select data. In this topic, you will learn how to select data in an Excel worksheet.

The following figures, Figure 1-5 and Figure 1-6, are two graphics of the same worksheet. You want to move the data in cell B3 to cell A3.

	A	B	C	D	E	F
1	Books and Beyond™ - Northeastern Region					
2						
3		5/9/2003				
4						
5		ID		January	February	March
6		123456789		175.65	140.96	135.15
7		234567890		210.63	240.82	205.79
8		345678901		185.11	195.14	310.44
9		456789012		195.37	215.97	350.15

Figure 1-5: *A worksheet before data is moved.*

	A	B	C	D	E	F
1	Books and Beyond™ - Northeastern Region					
2						
3	5/9/2003					
4						
5		ID		January	February	March
6		123456789		175.65	140.96	135.15
7		234567890		210.63	240.82	205.79
8		345678901		185.11	195.14	310.44
9		456789012		195.37	215.97	350.15

Figure 1-6: *A worksheet after data has been moved.*

To get the data from cell B3 (Figure 1-5) to cell A3 (Figure 1-6), you must first select the data in cell B3. Before you can manipulate any data that already exists in a worksheet, you must first know how to select that data.

How to Select Data

There are many ways to select data in an Excel worksheet. This table illustrates the most common methods for selecting data (see Table 1-4).

Table 1-4: *Ways to Select Data in Excel*

To Select	Do this
A single cell	Click the cell.
The contents of a cell	Do one of the following: • Double-click the cell to place the insertion point inside the cell, and then double-click again to select the contents of the cell. • Select the cell, and then select the contents of the Formula Bar.

To Select	Do this
A contiguous range of cells	Do one of the following: • Select the first cell in the contiguous range, navigate to the last cell in the range, press and hold Shift, and then click the last cell to select the full range. • Click and drag from the first cell to the last cell.
A discontiguous range of cells	Select the first cell in the range, navigate to the next cell in the range, press and hold Ctrl, and then click the cell. You can combine the Shift-click and Ctrl-click methods if necessary.
An entire worksheet	Click the blank box immediately below the Name Box.

ACTIVITY 1-3

Selecting Data

Objective:

To select data.

Setup:

The file NavigationPractice is open in Excel.

Scenario:

Continuing your reinforcement of basic concepts in Excel, you will now practice the different ways of selecting data in Excel.

What You Do	How You Do It
1. **Select a single cell containing data, and then select the data inside the cell.**	a. If necessary, **scroll up** to display cell D47. b. **Click cell D47** to select the cell.

c. **Double-click cell D47** to place the insertion point inside the cell.

d. **Double-click again in cell D47** to select the cell's data.

---

2. **Select a range of cells.**

a. **Select cell B38.**

b. **Press and hold Shift.**

c. **Click cell D41** to select all of the cells from B38 to D41.

33	Laura	Reagan	GBW77	Co
34	Brian	Smith	GS40	Ma
35	Mary	Barber	GW32	Ma
36	Peter	Allen	AW24	Ver
37	Mary	Altman	GC12	Ma
38	Fred	Mallory	CA06	Nev

---

3. **Select an entire worksheet.**

a. **Use the vertical scroll bar to scroll to the top of the worksheet.**

b. **Click the blank box immediately below the Name Box** to select the entire worksheet.

Click inside this box.

TOPIC D

Enter Data

You have worked with existing data in a worksheet. Now you would like to add your own data to a worksheet. In this topic, you will enter data into a worksheet.

Imagine you are a sales manager, and the vice president of sales has just asked you to make some projections for the upcoming year. Figure 1-7 and Figure 1-8 show two worksheets. Which worksheet helps you make business decisions for your sales group?

Figure 1-7: *A blank worksheet.*

	A	B	C	D	E
1	North American Division Sales Totals for Fiscal 2003				
2					
3	Item	QTR 1	QTR 2	QTR 3	QTR 4
4	Hardware	200	600	700	400
5	Software	300	200	500	600
6	Furniture	200	400	500	100
7	Accessories	300	300	100	200
8					
9	Totals:	$1,000	$1,500	$1,800	$1,300
10					
11					

Figure 1-8: *A worksheet containing useful data.*

Knowing how to enter data into a worksheet is the difference between using Excel to help you make sound business decisions and purchasing a software application you never use.

How to Enter Data

Procedure Reference: Enter Data

To enter data into an Excel spreadsheet:

1. Either create a new workbook or open an existing workbook.

2. Select the cell in which you want to enter data.

3. Type the data you want the cell to contain.

4. Either press Enter or Tab to place the data into the cell and move the insertion point to a new cell.

   - Press Enter to move down one cell.

   - Press Tab to move right one cell.

ACTIVITY 1-4

Entering Data

Objective:
To enter data.

Setup:
Close any workbooks that might be open (choose File→Close) without saving.

Scenario:
You just sat down at your desk to begin the day's work. Your manager hands you a handwritten paper spreadsheet that she wants you to enter into Excel, as shown in Figure 1-9. You will now enter this data into an Excel spreadsheet so that the Excel spreadsheet closely mirrors the layout of the paper spreadsheet.

			1	2	3	
	Months		Sales	Expenses	Totals	
1	Jan		120	115		
2	Feb		195	100		
3	Mar		230	125		
4						
5	Totals					
6						
7						
8						
9						
10						
11						
12						
13						

Figure 1-9: *The paper spreadsheet your manager has given to you.*

What You Do	How You Do It
1. Create a new, blank workbook.	a. Choose File→New.

b. In the New Workbook task pane, **click Blank Workbook** to open a new, blank workbook.

---

2. Enter *Months* as the column heading.

    a. **Double-click cell A1.**

    b. **Type *Months***

    c. **Press Enter.**

---

3. Enter the column headings *Sales*, *Expenses*, and *Totals*.

    a. **Select cell D1.**

    b. **Click in the Formula Bar.**

    c. **Type *Sales***

    d. **Press Tab.**

    e. **In cell E1, type *Expenses***

    f. **Press Tab.**

g. In cell F1, type *Totals*

	A	B	C	D	E	F
				▼ ✕ ✓ *f&* Totals		
1	Months			Sales	Expenses	Totals

---

4. **Enter the names of the months.**

a. **Select cell A3.**

b. **Click in the Formula Bar.**

c. **Type *Jan***

d. **Press Enter.**

e. In cell A4, **type *Feb* and press Enter.**

f. In cell A5, **type *Mar* and press Enter.**

	A	E
1	Months	
2		
3	Jan	
4	Feb	
5	Mar	
6		
7		

---

5. **Enter the sales values.**

a. **Select cell D3, type *120* and press Enter.**

b. In cell D4, **type *195* and press Enter.**

c. In cell D5, **type *230* and press Enter.**

D	E	F
Sales	Expenses	Totals
120		
195		
230		

---

6. **Enter the expense values.**

a. **Select cell E3, type *115* and press Enter.**

b. In cell E4, **type *100* and press Enter.**

c. In cell E5, **type *125* and press Enter.**

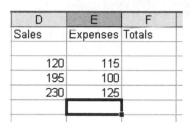

TOPIC E

Save a Workbook

You have entered data into a worksheet, and now you need to store that data so you can access it again and again. In this topic, you will save a workbook.

You have developed a complex workbook that helps you track sales data. If you don't save your workbook, when you turn your computer off, you will lose all of your work and not be able to access the workbook at a later date. By saving your work regularly, you make that work accessible beyond your current work session.

Save vs. Save As

Both the Save and Save As commands can be used to save a file to disk. However, the Save and Save As commands are used in slightly different situations.

Use Save when you want to:

*   Save a brand new file you've never saved before.
*   Resave an existing file and you do not need to change the file's name, type, or directory location.

Use Save As when you want to resave an existing file:

*   With a new name.
*   With a new file type.
*   In a new directory.

Don't be alarmed when you use the File→Save command or click the Save button to save a file for the first time and the Save As (instead of the Save) dialog box opens (see Figure 1-10). This only happens when you save a file that has never been saved before. The Save As dialog box opens because you are changing the name of the file from the default name (usually something like Book1) to a more appropriate name.

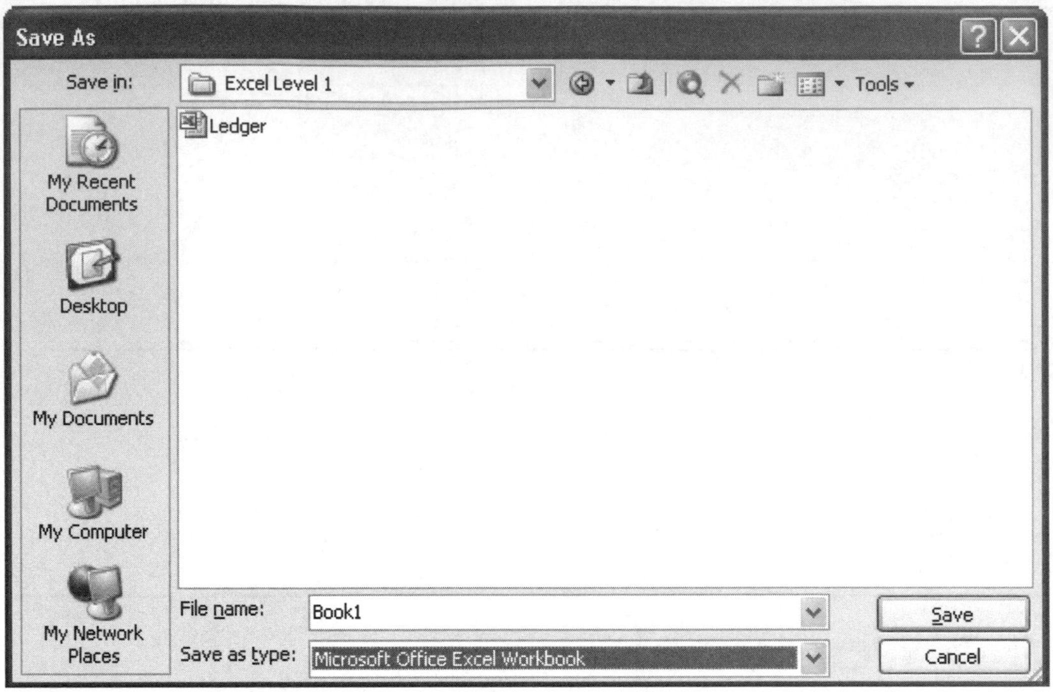

Figure 1-10: *The Save As dialog box.*

How to Save a Workbook

Procedure Reference: Save a New Workbook

To save a new workbook:

1. With a new workbook open in Excel, choose File→Save to open the Save As dialog box.

2. Navigate to the directory where you want to save the file.

3. Name the file.

4. Click Save.

Procedure Reference: Save an Existing Workbook with a New Name

To save an existing workbook, follow this steps:

1. With an existing workbook open in Excel, choose File→Save As to open the Save As dialog box.

2. Navigate to the directory where you want to save the file.

3. Rename the file.

4. Click Save.

ACTIVITY 1-5

Saving a Workbook

Objective:

To save a workbook.

Setup:

Activity 1-4 is complete and the unnamed file is still open in Excel.

Scenario:

You have just converted your manager's paper spreadsheet into an Excel file. You have not saved the file. Your manager has asked for two copies of the Excel file: one she can change and manipulate as needed and another one she wants to keep for safe storage. You have decided to name these files Ledger and Ledger_SAFE, respectively, and save them in a folder on your desktop.

What You Do	How You Do It
1. On the Windows desktop, **create a new folder.**	a. In Excel, **click the Minimize button.** 
	b. On the Windows desktop, **right-click and select New→Folder** to place a new folder on the desktop.
	c. **Type *ledgerFiles* and press Enter.**

2. **Save the file.**

    a. On the Windows taskbar, **click the Microsoft Excel - Book# button** to maximize Excel.

             start   Microsoft Excel - Book1

    b. **Choose File→Save** to open the Save As dialog box.

    c. **Click the Desktop icon** in the left pane of the Save As dialog box.

    d. **Double-click the ledgerFiles folder.**

    e. In the File Name text box, **click and drag to select the default file name.**

    f. **Press Delete.**

    g. In the File Name text box, **type** *Ledger*

             File name: Ledger

    h. **Click Save.**

3. **Save the file with a new name, and then close Excel.**

    a. **Choose File→Save As.**

    b. In the File Name text box, **type** *Ledger_SAFE*

             File name: Ledger_SAFE

    c. **Click Save.**

    d. **Choose File→Exit** to close Excel.

4. Locate the files on your computer's hard disk.	a. On the Windows desktop, **double-click the ledgerFiles folder** to view the contents of the folder in Windows Explorer.

Name ▲	Size	Type	Date Modified
Ledger	14 KB	Microsoft Excel Wor...	9/24/2003 10:20 AM
Ledger_SAFE	14 KB	Microsoft Excel Wor...	9/24/2003 10:20 AM

	b. **Locate the Ledger and Ledger_SAFE files, and then close the ledgerFiles folder window.**
5. On the Windows desktop, **rename the folder you created, and then start Excel.**	a. On the Windows desktop, **right-click the ledgerFiles folder, and then select Rename** to enable renaming of the folder.
	b. **Type *ToManager* and press Enter.**
	c. On the Windows taskbar, **click Start.**
	d. **Choose All Programs→Microsoft Office→ Microsoft Office Excel 2003.**

TOPIC F

Obtain Help

You have performed simple tasks in Excel. Inevitably, you will need to learn how to do other tasks while working in the application. In this topic, you will learn how to obtain help from within Excel.

You are working on a workbook and find yourself constantly using the mouse to navigate between cells. You prefer to use keyboard shortcuts as much as possible. As shown in Figure 1-11, by accessing the help system, you can find information that shows you how to move through a worksheet using keyboard shortcuts.

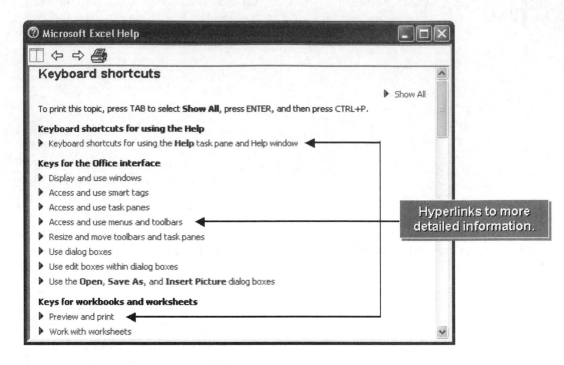

Figure 1-11: *Excel's help file illustrating keyboard shortcuts.*

How to Obtain Help

Procedure Reference: Obtain Help

To obtain help:

1. Choose Help→Microsoft Excel Help.

2. In the Search text box, type the subject of your search.

3. Click the Start Searching button.

4. Review the returned list of links, and then click the link that corresponds to your search.

Symbols

A symbol is a non-alphanumeric character that conveys information. Table 1-5 shows some examples of common symbols.

Table 1-5: *Examples of Symbols*

Symbol Name	Symbol
Copyright	©
Trademark	™
Registered	®

To insert symbols into a worksheet, select the cell that will contain the symbol, and then choose Insert→Symbol to open the Symbol dialog box. Select the symbol you want to insert, click Insert, and then click Close.

ACTIVITY 1-6

Obtaining Help

Objective:

To obtain help.

Data Files:

- HelpPractice

Setup:

Close any open files, but do not close Excel. Open the HelpPractice file.

Scenario:

You are working on a spreadsheet named HelpPractice that tracks employees and their roles in your organization. After reviewing your spreadsheet, your manager notices that the company name, CIRCA, is missing its trademark notice. She asks if it's possible for you to add the TM symbol to the company name. You tell your manager that you know it's possible, but that you aren't quite sure how to do it. You'll figure it out using Excel's Help system and then get the new copy to her.

What You Do	How You Do It

1. Search for and read the Help file for inserting symbols.

    a. Choose Help→Microsoft Excel Help.

    b. In the Search For text box, **type** *symbols*

Assistance

Search for:

`symbols|` →

Table of Contents

    c. **Click the Start Searching button** → .

    d. **Click the Insert A Symbol link** to open the Microsoft Excel Help dialog box and the Help file that explains how to insert a symbol.

Search Results ▼ ✕

← | → | ⌂

30 results from Office Online

Insert a symbol
Help > ...ering Data

Symbols for drawing object manipulation

    e. In the Microsoft Excel Help dialog box, **click the Insert A Symbol link** to expand the Insert A Symbol procedure.

② **Microsoft Excel Help** ⬜ ⬜ ✕

▯ ⇦ ⇨ 🖨

Insert a symbol

▸ Show All

You can use the **Symbol** dialog box to enter symbols that are not on your keyboard, as well as Unicode characters.

If you're using an expanded font, such as Arial or Times New Roman, the **Subset** list appears. Use this list to choose from an extended list of language characters, including Greek and Russian (Cyrillic), if available.

▸ Insert a symbol
▸ Insert a Unicode character

    f. **Read the Insert A Symbol procedure, and then close the Microsoft Excel Help**

dialog box.

2. **Add the TM symbol to the company name, and then save your work.**

a. With cell A1 selected, in the Formula Bar, **click immediately to the right of the "A" in "CIRCA"** so that there is no space between the "A" and the blinking cursor.

b. **Choose Insert→Symbol** to open the Symbol dialog box.

c. From the Subset drop-down list, **select Letterlike Symbols.**

d. **Select the TM symbol.**

e. **Click Insert** to insert the TM symbol.

f. **Click Close** to close the Symbol dialog box.

g. On the worksheet, **select any cell other than A1** to deselect cell A1.

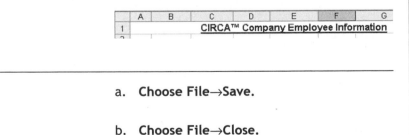

3. **Save and close the file.**

a. **Choose File→Save.**

b. **Choose File→Close.**

Lesson 1 Follow-up

In this lesson, you got started with Excel by familiarizing yourself with the Excel environment and interacting with some of its components. Because you have familiarized yourself with Excel, you can be a more efficient user.

1. **What projects are you currently working on that could benefit from incorporating Excel?**

2. **What are some of the benefits of using Excel in a business environment?**

LESSON 2
Modifying a Worksheet

Lesson Objectives:

In this lesson, you will modify a worksheet.

You will:

- Move and copy data between cells.
- Fill cells with series of data.
- Edit cell data.
- Insert and delete cells, columns, and rows.
- Find and replace cell data.
- Spell check a worksheet.

Introduction

You are now familiar with the Excel environment. After you've created a worksheet, you will undoubtedly want to make changes to that worksheet. In this lesson, you will modify the contents of a worksheet.

Your company has an existing worksheet that tracks sales reps and their data, as shown in Figure 2-1.

	A	B	C	D	E	F	G	H
1		Sales Team						
2								
3	Names		First Quarter			Second Quarter		
4	First Name	Last Name	Jan	Feb	Mar	Apr	May	Jun
5	Jane	Seeger	603.87	67.51	110	367.97	123.67	220.42
6	Phil	Egger	910.11	237.89	27.89	413.21	220.42	220.42
7	John	Wegman	220.42	220.42	367.89	213.41	603.87	67.51
8	Kim	Bennett	580.01	220.42	157.01	312.72	101.43	220.42
9								
10								

Figure 2-1: *The original Sales worksheet.*

The company has just hired a new sales rep.

Rather than create a new worksheet every time you need to change data, you can modify an existing worksheet to update your data, as shown in Figure 2-2.

	A	B	C	D
1		Sales Team		
2				
3	Names		First Quarter	
4	First Name	Last Name	Jan	Feb
5	Jane	Seeger	603.87	67.51
6	Phil	Egger	910.11	237.89
7	John	Wegman	220.42	220.42
8	Kim	Bennett	580.01	220.42
9	Josh	Langley	213.41	367.89
10				

New Sales Associate

Figure 2-2: *The modified Sales worksheet.*

TOPIC A

Move and Copy Data Between Cells

You have entered data and saved it in a workbook. Now you want to begin manipulating the data you have entered. In this topic, you will move and copy data between cells.

You are in the process of updating an expense worksheet with your most recent expenses. You've already entered "New Hotel" in the Description column for January 10th, as shown in Figure 2-3.

Employee				

Name	Ivana Buhreeto		Emp #	
SSN	123-45-6789		Position	
Department			Manager	

Date	Account	Description	Lodging	T
1/10/2003	North	New Hotel	$ 157.89	
1/11/2003	North			
1/12/2003	North			
1/13/2003	Carolina			
1/14/2003	Adiron			
1/15/2003	Dacks			
1/16/2003	Maple			
1/17/2003	Maple			

Figure 2-3: *An expense worksheet that contains data you would like to reuse.*

Now, you want "New Hotel" to appear in the Description column for January 17th and January 23rd, as shown in Figure 2-4.

Date	Account	Description	Lodging	Tr
1/10/2003	North	New Hotel	$ 157.89	
1/11/2003	North			
1/12/2003	North			
1/13/2003	Carolina			
1/14/2003	Adiron			
1/15/2003	Dacks			
1/16/2003	Maple			
1/17/2003	Maple	New Hotel	$ 189.63	
1/18/2003	Maple			
1/19/2003	Southern			
1/20/2003	Blue			
1/21/2003	Northern			
1/22/2003	Idita			
1/23/2003	Rodrace	New Hotel	$ 89.98	
1/24/2003				
1/25/2003				

Figure 2-4: *An expense worksheet with that data that has been copied to new cells.*

You can move or copy data you want to reuse—rather than retyping that data.

How to Move and Copy Data Between Cells

Procedure Reference: Move Data Between Cells

To move data between cells:

1. Select the contents of the cell that contains the data you want to move.

2. Cut the contents of the cell to the clipboard.

To cut the contents, select the contents of the cell and then do one of the following:

- Choose Edit→Cut.
- Click the Cut button ✂ .
- Press Ctrl+X.

3. Select the cell that you want to move the data to.

4. Paste the contents of the clipboard into the destination cell.

To paste the contents of the clipboard into the new cell, select the new cell and then do one of the following:

- Choose Edit→Paste.
- Click the Paste button 📋 .
- Press Ctrl+V.

Procedure Reference: Copy Data Between Cells

To copy data between cells:

1. Select the contents of the cell that contains the data you want to copy.

2. Copy the contents of the cell to the clipboard.

To copy the contents of the cell, select the contents of the cell and then do one of the following:

- Choose Edit→Copy.
- Click the Copy button 📋 .
- Press Ctrl+C.

3. Select the cell that you want to copy the data to.

4. Paste the contents of the clipboard into the destination cell.

ACTIVITY 2-1

Moving and Copying Data Between Cells

Objective:

To move and copy data between cells.

Data Files:

- Editing

Setup:

If any Excel files are open, close them. If the task pane is open, close it. Open the Editing file.

Scenario:

You have developed a worksheet that tracks sales data, and you have presented a draft copy of the worksheet to your manager for her review, as shown in Figure 2-5.

	A	B	C	D	E	F	G	H	I	J	K
1	Books and Beyond© - Northeastern Region										
2		5/15/2002									
3											
4		ID	January	February	March	April			Totals		
5		123456789	110.25	175.65	140.96	135.15					
6		234567890	200.75	210.63	240.82	205.79					
7		345678901	210.35	185.11	195.14	310.44					
8		456789012	220.15	195.37	185.66	250.15					
9											
10											
11	Books and Beyond - Mideastern Region										
12	5/15/2002										
13											
14		ID	January	February	March						
15		567890123	235	269.33	291.15	205.17					
16		678901234	115.6	110.7	133.5	147					
17		789012345	257.3	225	264.75	295.44					
18		890123456	189.1	240.7	223.5	123.08					
19											
20											
21											
22											
23											
24											

Figure 2-5: *Your draft copy of the Editing file.*

She likes what you have done, but has a few requests.

- Move the "Totals" heading one cell to the left.
- Move the date text for the Northeastern Region one cell to the left.
- Copy the "April" heading down to the Mideastern section.
- Copy the "Totals" heading down to the Mideastern section.

What You Do	How You Do It
1. Move the "Totals" heading one cell to the left.	a. Select cell I4.
	b. Choose Edit→Cut.
	c. Select cell H4.
	d. Choose Edit→Paste.
2. Move the date text for the Northeastern Region one cell to the left.	a. Select cell B2.
	b. **Point the mouse pointer at the black border around the cell** until the mouse pointer changes to a large arrow with a smaller, four-directional arrow.
	5/15/2002
	c. **Click and drag to cell A2.**
3. Copy "April" to the Mideastern Region.	a. Select cell F4.
	b. Choose Edit→Copy.
	c. Select cell F14.
	d. Choose Edit→Paste.
4. Copy "Totals" to the Mideastern Region, and then save your work.	a. Select cell H4.
	b. Choose Edit→Copy.
	c. Select cell H14.
	d. Choose Edit→Paste.
	e. Choose File→Save.

TOPIC B

Fill Cells with Series of Data

You have entered data into cells. You would now like to enter incremental data in rows and columns of cells. In this topic, you will fill cells with a series of data.

You are in the process of creating a worksheet that will act as a calendar, but you don't want to type in every month of the year. You've already entered January in cell A1, as shown in Figure 2-6. Without typing the words, you can fill cells B1 through L1 with the months February through December, respectively, as shown in Figure 2-7.

	A	B	C	D
1	January			
2				
3				
4				

Figure 2-6: *A worksheet with the month January in cell A1.*

	A	B	C	D	E	F	G	H	I	J	K	L
1	January	February	March	April	May	June	July	August	September	October	November	December
2												
3												

Figure 2-7: *A worksheet with all of the months of the year entered in series.*

By filling cells with series data, you don't have to type by hand all of the data that can automatically be generated by Excel.

AutoFill

The *AutoFill* feature fills a selected range of cells with a series of data. You enter data in one or more cells and drag a *fill handle* to other cells, without having to key in any additional information, as shown in Figure 2-8. Excel makes some assumptions when you enter the starting value(s) for the series you want to fill the cells with. Depending on the type of data (text or numeric) you're entering, you may only have to enter data in one cell for Excel to interpret the type of series you want to fill.

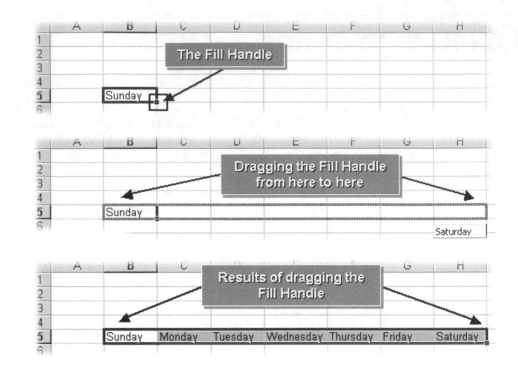

Figure 2-8: *AutoFill and the fill handle.*

How to Fill Cells with Series of Data

Procedure Reference: Fill Cells with a Series of Data Where the Starting Value Has Already Been Entered

To fill cells with a series of data where the starting value has already been entered:

1. Select the cell that contains the starting value of the series.

2. Click and drag the fill handle to the ending cell of the series.

Procedure Reference: Fill Cells with a Series of Data Where the Starting Value Has Not Yet Been Entered

To fill cells with a series of data where the starting value has not yet been entered:

1. Select the cell that will contain the starting value of the series.

2. Enter the starting value of the series.

3. Click and drag the fill handle to the ending cell of the series.

ACTIVITY 2-2

Filling Cells with a Series of Data

Objective:

To fill cells with a series of data.

Setup:

Activity 2-1 is complete. The file Editing is open.

Scenario:

You have developed a worksheet that tracks sales data, and you have presented a draft copy of the worksheet to your manager for her review, as shown in Figure 2-9.

	A	B	C	D	E	F	G	H	I
1	Books and Beyond© - Northeastern Region								
2	5/15/2002								
3									
4		ID	January	February	March	April		Totals	
5		123456789	110.25	175.65	140.96	135.15			
6		234567890	200.75	210.63	240.82	205.79			
7		345678901	210.35	185.11	195.14	310.44			
8		456789012	220.15	195.37	185.66	250.15			
9									
10									
11	Books and Beyond - Mideastern Region								
12	5/15/2002								
13									
14		ID	January	February	March	April		Totals	
15		567890123	235	269.33	291.15	205.17			
16		678901234	115.6	110.7	133.5	147			
17		789012345	257.3	225	264.75	295.44			
18		890123456	189.1	240.7	223.5	123.08			
19									
20									
21									
22									
23									
24									

Figure 2-9: *Your draft copy of the Editing file.*

Your manager notes that your draft meets the requirements she requested, but now the requirements have changed slightly, and she'd like you to revise the worksheet.

- Move the "Totals" column to column "P."
- Add the remaining months of the year for both the Northeastern and Mideastern Regions.

Lesson 2

What You Do	How You Do It
1. Move the Totals column.	a. Click the column H heading.

b. Choose Edit→Cut.

c. Click the column P heading.

d. Choose Edit→Paste.

2. Add the remaining months of the year for the Northeastern Region.	a. Select cell F4.

b. Click and drag the fill handle to cell N4 to fill the corresponding cells with the remaining months of the year.

3. Add the remaining months of the year for the Mideastern Region, and then save your work.	a. Select cell F14.

b. Click and drag the fill handle to cell N14 to fill the corresponding cells with the remaining months of the year.

c. Choose File→Save.

4. Which are good candidates for AutoFill?

a) Adding Q1 through Q4 as headings for fiscal quarters.

b) Adding the days of the week.

c) Adding employee sales totals.

d) Adding the consecutive years 1990 through 2003.

TOPIC C

Edit Cell Data

You have modified worksheets by adding, moving, and copying data. You now need to alter the existing contents of some cells. In this topic, you will edit cell data.

You just entered the text "Account" in your worksheet, as shown in Figure 2-10. You meant to enter the text "Names." You can change the text so that it now reads "Names," as shown in Figure 2-11.

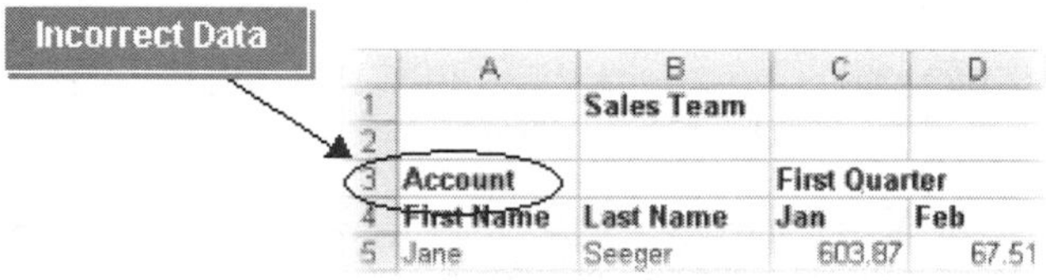

Figure 2-10: *A cell containing incorrect data.*

Figure 2-11: *An edited cell that contains corrected data.*

By editing cell data as needed, you ensure data integrity. Additionally, by editing cell data, you don't need to recreate an entirely new worksheet with the correct data.

Undo and Redo

Undo allows you to reverse one or more of your most recent actions. Redo allows you to cancel one or more of your most recent Undo actions. The Undo and Redo commands can be found on the Edit menu.

Suppose you're clearing the contents of a cell, and you realize that you deleted the wrong data. You can use the Undo command to reverse your last action. What if you enter some text in a cell, choose Undo because you decide you don't want that text, and then you realize that you really do want the text? You can use the Redo command to cancel your last Undo action.

Not all actions can be undone in Excel. For example, you cannot undo a File→Save.

How to Edit Cell Data

Procedure Reference: Edit Cell Data

To edit cell data:

1. Select the contents of the cell that contains the data you want to edit.

2. Type the new value into the cell.

3. Exit the edited cell.

Activity 2-3

Editing Cell Data

Objective:

To edit cell data.

Setup:

Activity 2-2 is complete. The file Editing is open.

Scenario:

The following figure, Figure 2-12, shows a worksheet you have developed that tracks sales data, and you have presented a draft copy of the worksheet to your manager for her review.

	A	B	C	D	E	F	G	H	I	J	K	L	M	N	O	P
1	Books and Beyond© - Northeastern Region															
2	5/15/2002															
3																
4		ID	January	February	March	April	May	June	July	August	September	October	November	December		Totals
5		123456789	110.25	175.65	140.96	135.15										
6		234567890	200.75	210.63	240.82	205.79										
7		345678901	210.35	185.11	195.14	310.44										
8		456789012	220.15	195.37	185.66	250.15										
9																
10																
11	Books and Beyond - Mideastern Region															
12	5/15/2002															
13																
14		ID	January	February	March	April	May	June	July	August	September	October	November	December		Totals
15		567890123	235	269.33	291.15	205.17										
16		678901234	115.6	110.7	133.5	147										
17		789012345	257.3	225	264.75	295.44										
18		890123456	189.1	240.7	223.5	123.08										

Figure 2-12: *Your draft copy of the Editing file.*

Your manager notes that your draft meets the requirements she requested, but some of the data you entered is slightly incorrect.

- The April total for ID number 456789012 should be 350.15, not 250.15.
- The cells with "5/15/2002" should read "Fiscal 2003."
- "Mideastern region" should be "Midwestern region."
- The copyright symbol (©) should be the trademark symbol (™).

LESSON 2

What You Do	How You Do It

1. **Edit the April value for ID 456789012.**

a. **Select cell F8** so that the Formula Bar will display the contents of the cell.

fx 250.15		
F	G	H
April	May	June
96 135.15		
82 205.79		
14 310.44		
66 250.15		

b. In the Formula Bar, **click and drag to select its contents.**

c. In the Formula Bar, **type *350.15***

d. **Press Enter.**

195.14	310.44
185.66	350.15

2. **Change "5/15/2002" to *Fiscal 2003*.**

a. **Double-click cell A2** to place the insertion point inside the cell.

b. **Double-click inside cell A2** to select the contents of the cell.

c. **Type *Fiscal 2003* and press Enter.**

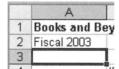

A
1 Books and Bey
2 Fiscal 2003
3

d. **Double-click cell A12** to place the insertion point inside the cell.

e. **Double-click inside cell A12** to select the contents of the cell.

f. **Type *Fiscal 2003* and press Enter.**

LESSON 2

3. Change "Mideastern" to *Midwest-ern*

    a. Select cell A11.

    b. Type *Midwestern* and press Enter.

    c. You realize you have accidently deleted most of the contents of the cell, so you **choose Edit→Undo Typing 'Midwestern' In A11.**

    d. In the Formula Bar, **click and drag to select the word "Mideastern."**

    e. Type *Midwestern* and press Enter.

---

4. Consider the following: Your manager asks you to clear a range of data in a worksheet. You do so, but then a short while later your manager returns to say he has made a mistake. He actually wants to keep the data you just deleted. Which action would most quickly return the deleted data to the worksheet?

    a) Undo

    b) Clear

    c) Redo

    d) Edit

---

5. Change the copyright symbol (©) to the trademark symbol (™), and then save your work.

    a. Select cell A1.

    b. In the Formula Bar, **click and drag to select the copyright symbol (©).**

    c. **Press Delete.**

    d. **Choose Insert→Symbol.**

    e. From the Subset drop-down list, **select Letterlike Symbols.**

f. **Double-click the trademark symbol (™) to insert the trademark symbol into the cell.**

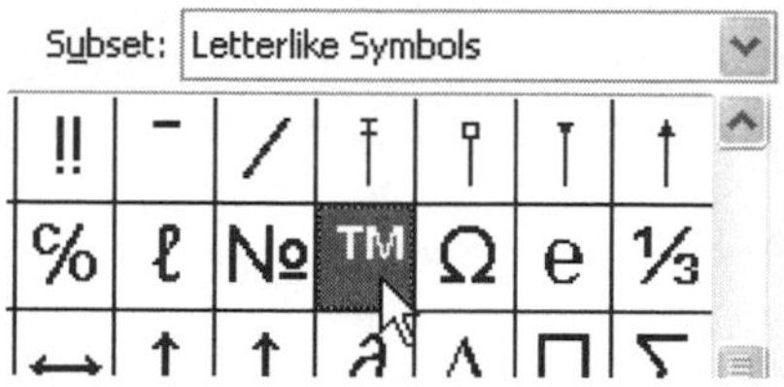

g. In the Symbol dialog box, **click Close.**

h. **Choose File→Save.**

TOPIC D

Insert and Delete Cells, Columns, and Rows

You have entered data into cells, and you have filled cells with a series of data. Now, you want to alter the number of cells, columns, and rows in a worksheet to accommodate changes in your data. In this topic, you will insert and delete cells, columns, and rows.

The following figure, Figure 2-13, shows the first draft of an expense statement workbook you have created for your manager.

Figure 2-13: *The first draft of an expense statement workbook.*

After reviewing your draft, your manager has requested some changes. The following figure, Figure 2-14, shows the changes you have made to the workbook.

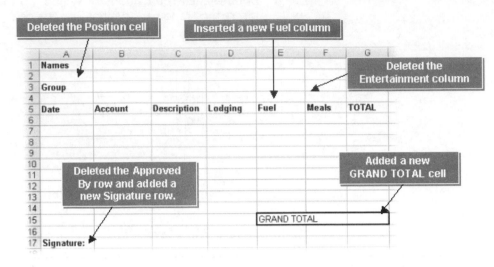

Figure 2-14: *The second draft of an expense statement workbook.*

By inserting and deleting cells, columns, and rows, you can modify the layout of a single workbook rather than create a new workbook every time your data requirements change.

How to Insert and Delete Cells, Columns, and Rows

Procedure Reference: Insert Rows

To insert rows:

1.   Click the row heading of the row that will shift below the new row.

2.   Choose Insert→Rows to insert the new row and shift all other rows downward.

Procedure Reference: Insert Columns

To insert columns:

1.   Click the column heading of the column that will move to the right of the new column.

2.   Choose Insert→Columns to insert the new column and shift all other columns to the right.

Procedure Reference: Insert Cells

To insert cells:

1.   Click the existing cell that you would like to insert a cell next to.

2.   Choose Insert→Cells.

3.   In the Insert dialog box, select the appropriate option, and then click OK to insert the new cell. The following are the options available in the Insert dialog box:

     •   Shift Cells Right.

     •   Shift Cells Down.

     •   Entire Row.

     •   Entire Column.

Procedure Reference: Delete Cells, Rows, and Columns

To delete cells, rows, and columns:

1. Select the existing cell, row, or column that you want to delete.

2. Choose Edit→Delete.

   Columns and rows will delete automatically.

   If you have selected a cell for deletion, the Delete dialog box will open with these options:
   - Shift Cells Left.
   - Shift Cells Up.
   - Entire Row.
   - Entire Column.

3. If the Delete dialog box is open, select which option you want to delete, and then click OK.

ACTIVITY 2-4

Inserting and Deleting Cells, Columns, and Rows

Objective:

To insert and delete cells, columns, and rows.

Setup:

Activity 2-3 is complete. The file Editing is open.

Scenario:

You have developed a worksheet that tracks sales data, and you have presented a draft copy of the worksheet to your manager for her review, as shown in Figure 2-15.

Books and Beyond™ - Northeastern Region														
Fiscal 2003														
	ID	January	February	March	April	May	June	July	August	September	October	November	December	Totals
	123456789	110.25	175.65	140.96	135.15									
	234567890	200.75	210.63	240.82	205.79									
	345678901	210.35	185.11	195.14	310.44									
	456709012	220.15	195.37	185.66	350.15									
Books and Beyond - Midwestern Region														
Fiscal 2003														
	ID	January	February	March	April	May	June	July	August	September	October	November	December	Totals
	567890123	235	269.33	291.15	205.17									
	678901234	115.6	110.7	133.5	147									
	789012345	257.3	225	264.75	295.44									
	890123456	189.1	240.7	223.5	123.08									

Figure 2-15: *Your draft copy of the Editing file.*

Your manager notes that your draft meets the requirements she requested, but she has some further changes she would like to make to the worksheet.

- Insert two rows above the current row 1.

- Insert one column before the current column A.
- Insert a block of cells between the ID data and the January data for each region.
- Delete content from the two rows that begin with "Fiscal 2003."
- Delete the empty column between the December and Totals headings.
- Delete the January totals (not the January heading) for each ID, and shift the other monthly total columns one cell to the left.

What You Do	How You Do It
1. **Insert two rows above the current row 1.**	a. **Click the row 1 row heading** to select the entire row.
	b. **Choose Insert→Rows** to insert a new row.
	c. **Choose Insert→Rows** again to insert a second new row.
2. **Insert a new column before column A.**	a. **Click the column A heading** to select the entire column.
	b. **Choose Insert→Columns** to insert a new column to the left of the existing column A.

3. For each region, **insert a block of cells between the ID data and the January data.**

a. **Select cell D6.**

b. **Press and hold Shift, and then click cell D10** to select cells D6 through D10.

	January	F
39	110.25	
30	200.75	
11	210.35	
2	220.15	

c. **Press and hold Ctrl, and then click cells D16, D17, D18, D19, and D20** to select cells D16 through D20.

	January	Fel
9	110.25	
0	200.75	
1	210.35	
2	220.15	

stern Region

	January	Fel
3	235	
4	115.6	
5	257.3	
6	189.1	

d. **Choose Insert→Cells** to open the Insert dialog box with the Shift Cells Right option selected by default.

e. **Click OK** to insert the new cells.

4. **Delete the phrase "Fiscal 2003" from rows 4 and 14.**

a. **Click the row 4 row heading** to select the row.

b. **Press and hold Ctrl, and then click the row 14 row heading** to select rows 4 and 14.

c. **Choose Edit→Delete** to delete "Fiscal 2003" from rows 4 and 14.

5. **Delete the empty column between the December and Totals headings.**

    a. **Click the column Q heading** to select the entire column.

    b. To delete the existing column Q and automatically shift all of the columns to the right of column Q to the left, **choose Edit→Delete.**

---

6. **Delete the January totals for each ID, shift the remaining monthly totals one cell to the left, and then save your work.**

    a. **Select cell E6.**

    b. **Press and hold Shift, and then click cell E9** to select cells E6 through E9.

    c. **Press and hold Ctrl, and then click cells E15, E16, E17, and E18** to select cells E6 through E9 and E15 through E18.

    d. **Choose Edit→Delete** to open the Delete dialog box with the Shift Cells Left option selected by default.

    e. **Click OK** to delete the selected cells and shift the values from February through March one cell to the left.

    f. **Choose File→Save.**

TOPIC E

Find, Replace, and Go To Cell Data

You have your data in your worksheet. You now have a need to locate and change the data in specific cells. In this topic, you will find and replace cell data.

You just realized that a piece of data in your worksheet is incorrect. You could search for the data by visually examining each cell starting from the beginning of the worksheet, but that would take a lot of time. Instead, you can use Find And Replace to locate and change the incorrect data.

In large worksheets, Find And Replace is much faster than manually locating the data. Additionally, if other instances of the same data exist that you didn't know about, you can change their value at the same time.

Find

The Find command locates specific data within a worksheet. To access the Find command, do one of the following:

* Choose Edit→Find.

* Press Ctrl+F.

Either of these actions opens the Find And Replace dialog box.

The Find Next button locates the next instance of the search criteria. The Find All button locates every instance of the search criteria and populates a list of hyperlinks at the bottom of the Find and Replace dialog box. Figure 2-16 and Figure 2-17 show the Find And Replace dialog box.

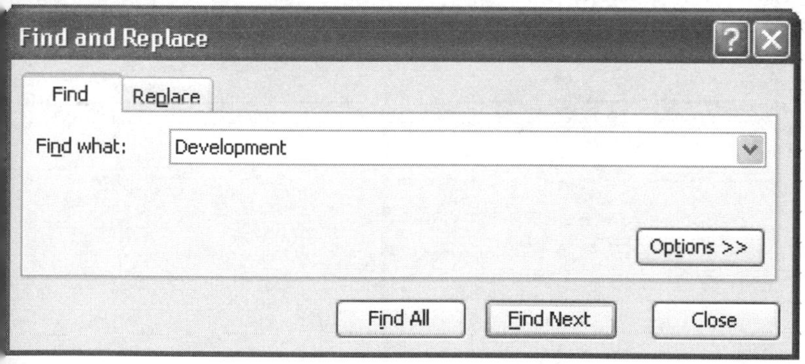

Figure 2-16: *The Find And Replace dialog box after clicking the Find Next button.*

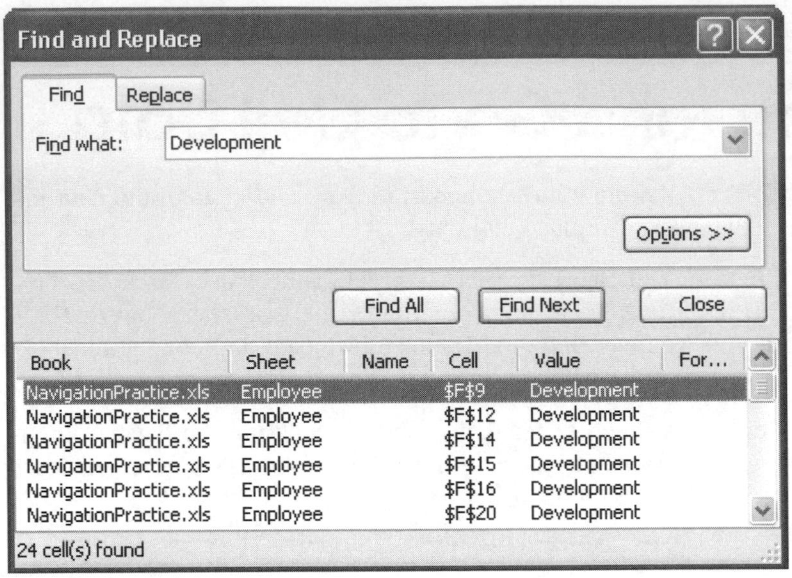

Figure 2-17: *The Find And Replace dialog box after clicking the Find All button.*

Replace

The Replace command replaces existing data within a worksheet with new data you have specified. To access Replace, do one of the following:

- Choose Edit→Replace.
- Press Ctrl+H.

Either of these actions opens the Find And Replace dialog box.

The Replace button replaces the selected instance of the search criteria. The Replace All button replaces every instance of the search criteria with the new data Figure 2-18 shows the Replace and Replace All buttons in the Find And Replace dialog box.

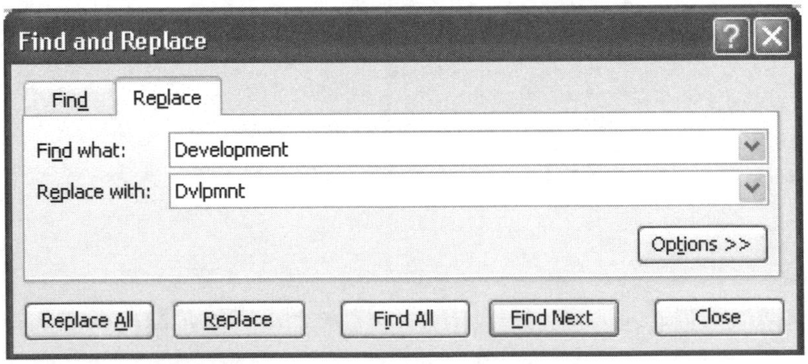

Figure 2-18: *The Find And Replace dialog box.*

Cell Names

Definition:

A cell name is a name that identifies a cell by a term you specify, rather than by the cell's column and row identification (A32, B17, and so on). You can apply names to a cell or a range of cells. Cell names provide context to cell content, making it easier to locate information in a worksheet.

Example: A Cell Name

A cell name appears in the Name Box when the cell is selected, as shown in Figure 2-19.

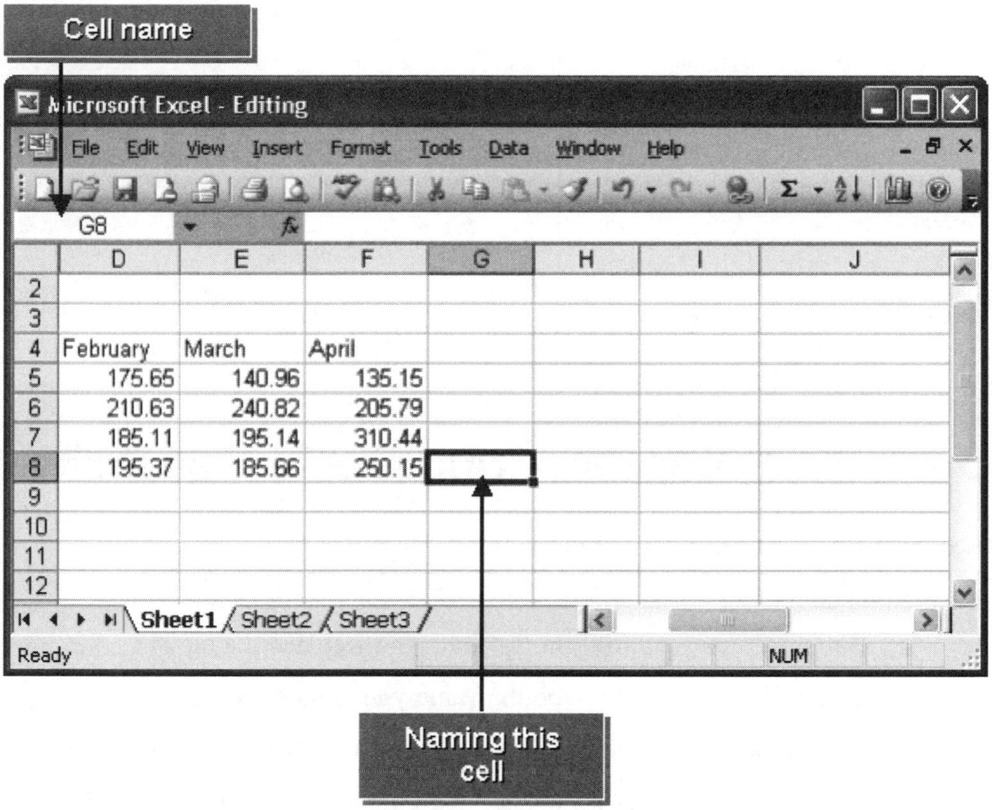

Figure 2-19: *A cell name in the Name Box.*

Go To

The Go To command takes you to a specific cell either by a cell reference (such as A2) or by a cell name you have specified. To access Go To, do one of the following:

- Choose Edit→Go To.
- Press Ctrl+G.

Either of these actions opens the Go To dialog box, as shown in Figure 2-20.

Figure 2-20: *The Go To dialog box.*

How to Find, Replace, and Go To Cell Data

Procedure Reference: Find Cell Data

To find cell data:

1. Choose Edit→Find to open the Find And Replace dialog box.

2. In the Find What field, type the value you want to find.

3. Click Find Next to find each instance of the value in the workbook.

4. In the Find And Replace dialog box, click Close when you are finished.

Procedure Reference: Replace Cell Data

To replace cell data:

1. Choose Edit→Replace to open the Find And Replace dialog box.

2. In the Find What field, type the value you want to find.

    ✎ You can press Tab to advance from the Find What field to the Replace With field.

3. In the Replace With field, type the new value that will replace the existing value.

4. Click Find Next to find each instance of the value in the workbook.

5. Click Replace to replace any instance you want to change.

6. In the Find And Replace dialog box, click Close when you are finished.

Procedure Reference: Go to Specific Cell Data

To replace cell data:

1. Choose Edit→Go To to open the Go To dialog box.

2. From the Go To list, select the name of the cell you want to go to, or type the cell reference in the Reference field.

3. Click OK to go to the cell and close the Go To dialog box.

ACTIVITY 2-5

Finding, Replacing, and Going to Cell Data

Objective:

To find, replace, and go to cell data.

Setup:

Activity 2-4 is complete. The file Editing is open.

Scenario:

After reviewing your draft of the sales data worksheet, your manager realizes she has given you some incorrect information.

- Employee 789012345 should have a March total of 314.04, not 295.44.
- Employee 456789012 should have a February total of 215.97, not 185.66.

Additionally, your manager has also asked if you can make it easy for her to find the totals columns for each region.

As you begin work on editing the worksheet, your manager calls and asks, "Which employee had the $269.33 sales total for February?" You use the Find command to locate this information for your manager.

What You Do	How You Do It
1. With cell A1 selected, **find the value 269.33.**	a. With cell A1 selected, **choose Edit→Find** to open the Find And Replace dialog box.
	b. In the Find What field, **type 269.33**
	c. **Click Find Next** to locate the cell containing the data.
	d. In the Find And Replace dialog box, **click Close.**

2. **Find the March total for Employee 789012345 and replace it with the correct value.**

   a. Choose Edit→**Replace** to open the Find And Replace dialog box.

   b. **Click and drag to select the contents of the Find What field, and then type** *295.44*

   c. **Press Tab to advance to the Replace With field, and then type** *314.04*

Fin**d**	Re**p**lace
Fi**n**d what:	295.44
Re**p**lace with:	314.04

   d. **Click Find Next.**

   e. **Click Replace.**

3. **Find the February total for Employee 456789012 and replace it with the correct value.**

   a. In the Find And Replace dialog box, **click and drag to select the contents of the Find What field, and then type** *185.66*

   b. **Click and drag to select the contents of the Replace With field, and then type** *215.97*

Fin**d**	Re**p**lace
Fi**n**d what:	185.66
Re**p**lace with:	215.97

   c. **Click Find Next.**

   d. **Click Replace.**

   e. In the Find And Replace dialog box, **click Close.**

4. **Name the Totals cells.**

   a. **Select cell Q5.**

b. **Click in the Name Box, and then type** *netotals*

c. **Press Enter** to name the cell.

d. **Select cell Q14.**

e. **Click in the Name Box, and then type** *mwtotals*

f. **Press Enter** to name the cell.

---

5. **Go to one of the Totals cells, and then save your work.**

a. In the Name Box, **type** *A1* **and press Enter** to navigate back to cell A1.

b. **Choose Edit→Go To** to open the Go To dialog box.

c. In the Go To box, **select mwtotals, and then click OK** to go to the Totals cell for the Midwestern Region.

d. **Choose File→Save.**

TOPIC F

Spell Check a Worksheet

You have revised your worksheet data. Now you want to make sure all of the text in the worksheet is spelled correctly. In this topic, you will spell check a worksheet.

You are working on your expense worksheet. As a final step in the process before you submit it to your manager, you want to verify the spelling of the text in the file. By spell checking your worksheet, you can correct any misspelled words.

How to Spell Check a Worksheet

Procedure Reference: Spell Check a Worksheet

To spell check a worksheet:

1. With a workbook open in Excel, choose Tools→Spelling to open the Spelling dialog box. The spell checker will automatically advance to the first word it does not recognize.

2. If necessary, to correct misspelled words:

    *   When the correct version of the word appears in the Suggestions list, select the correct word from the Suggestions list and then click Change.

    *   When the correct version of the word does not appear in the Suggestions list, type the correct version of the word in the Not In Dictionary field, and then click Change.

ACTIVITY 2-6

Spell Checking a Worksheet

Objective:
To spell check a worksheet.

Data Files:

*   Spelling

Setup:
Close any open files. Open the file Spelling.

Scenario:
You have just completed developing a travel expenses worksheet for your manager. Before you submit the worksheet to your manager, you have decided to spell check the contents of the worksheet and fix any misspelled words.

What You Do	How You Do It
1. Spell check the Spelling file.	a. **Choose Tools→Spelling** to open the Spelling dialog box and identify the first misspelled word.
	b. **Click Change** to replace the misspelled word with its correction and automatically advance to the next misspelled word.
	c. **Click Change** to complete the spell checking process.
	d. In the message dialog box, **click OK** to confirm the completion of the spell checking process.
2. Save and close your work.	a. **Choose File→Save.**
	b. **Choose File→Close.**

Lesson 2 Follow-up

In this lesson, you modified a worksheet by moving and copying data between cells. You filled cells with series data, and you practiced editing the data stored in cells. You learned how to insert and delete cells, rows, and columns, and you practiced finding, replacing, and going to data. Finally, you used Excel's spell checker to spell check the contents of a worksheet.

1. **You have done some basic modifications to a worksheet. Consider a worksheet you are either already using at work or one you need to create from scratch. How might you modify the existing worksheet (the former situation) or Excel's default worksheet (the latter situation) to meet your current business needs?**

2. **What spreadsheets or worksheets have you seen that are particularly well designed? How might you incorporate some of those design ideas into a project you are currently working on or are about to start?**

NOTES

LESSON 3
Performing Calculations

Lesson Objectives:

In this lesson, you will perform calculations.

You will:

- Create basic formulas.
- Calculate with functions.
- Copy formulas and functions.
- Create an absolute reference.

Introduction

You've entered data into a worksheet and you've modified a worksheet to meet your business needs. Now you need to generate new data based on the data you've already entered. You can do this by performing calculations on the existing data.

The following figure, Figure 3-1, shows a spreadsheet containing sales data. Your manager has asked you for the total sales for all reps for the month of February. Would you like to calculate this by hand?

	A	B	C	D	E	F	G
1	Books and Beyond - Northeastern Region						
2	5/15/2002						
3							
4							
5		Employee ID	January	February	March	April	
6							
7		123456789	110.25	175.65	140.96	135.15	
8		234567890	200.75	210.63	240.82	205.79	
9		345678901	210.34	185.11	195.14	310.44	
10		456789012	220.15	195.37	185.66	250.15	
11							
12							
13							

Figure 3-1: *A spreadsheet containing sales data.*

Calculating by hand is inefficient. Excel can do this for you.

TOPIC A

Create Basic Formulas

You are ready to run calculations on your data. The first way to do this is with a basic formula. In this topic, you will create basic formulas.

You have a worksheet that contains sales data, as shown in Figure 3-2. You want to find the average sale amount for each employee. A formula can calculate this average for you, as shown in Figure 3-3.

	A	B	C	D	E	F	G	H	
1	Books and Beyond - Northeastern Region								
2	5/15/2003								
3						Commission Rate:		17%	
4									
5		Employee ID	January	February	March	April		YTD Average	
6									
7		123456789	110.25	175.65	140.96	135.15			
8		234567890	200.75	210.63	240.82	205.79			
9		345678901	210.34	185.11	195.14	310.44			
10		456789012	220.15	195.37	185.66	250.15			
11									
12		Monthly Totals							
13		Monthly Average							
14									
15									
16									

Figure 3-2: *A sales worksheet with no calculations.*

	A	B	C	D	E	F	G	H	
1	Books and Beyond - Northeastern Region								
2	5/15/2003								
3						Commission Rate:		17%	
4									
5		Employee ID	January	February	March	April		YTD Average	
6									
7		123456789	110.25	175.65	140.96	135.15		140.50	
8		234567890	200.75	210.63	240.82	205.79		214.50	
9		345678901	210.34	185.11	195.14	310.44		225.26	
10		456789012	220.15	195.37	185.66	250.15		212.83	
11									
12		Monthly Totals							
13		Monthly Average							
14									

Figure 3-3: *A sales worksheet that calculates averages.*

Creating basic formulas helps you cull valuable information from the data you've entered into a worksheet.

Formulas

Definition:

A *formula* is a set of mathematical instructions that performs calculations. Formulas can contain any mathematically sound combination of numbers and symbols.

Some common mathematical symbols include:

- The plus sign (+) for addition.
- The minus sign (–) for subtraction.
- The asterisk (*) for multiplication.
- The front slash (/) for division.
- The caret symbol (^) for exponents.
- The open and close parentheses ( ) to group computation instructions.

Example: A Formula

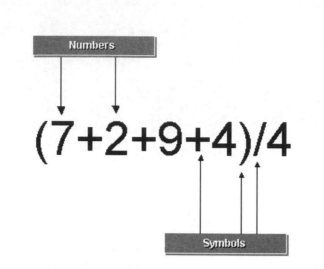

Order of Operations

Definition:

An *order of operations* is a sequence of computations that a formula follows to arrive at a desired result. The order of operations follows this sequence:

1. Computations enclosed in parentheses are performed first, no matter where they appear in the formula.

2. Computations involving exponents are performed second.

3. Computations involving multiplication and division are performed third. Because they are equal with regard to the order in which Excel performs them, Excel performs them in the order in which it encounters them (from left to right).

4. Computations involving addition and subtraction are performed last. Excel also performs them in the order in which it encounters them (from left to right).

Example: The Order of Operations at Work

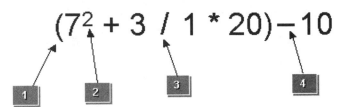

$$(7^2 + 3 / 1 * 20) - 10$$

1 2 3 4

Order of Operations

1. Computations with parentheses

2. Computations with exponents

3. Computations with multiplication or division

4. Computations with addition or subtraction

How to Create Basic Formulas

Procedure Reference: Create a Basic Formula

To create a basic formula:

1. Select the cell in which you would like the formula to appear.

2. In the Formula Bar, type an equal sign, and then type the formula you would like to perform.

3. Press Enter.

Formulas in Excel

In Excel, all formulas begin with an equal sign (=). Additionally, you can write formulas using cell references rather than numbers. If cell A1 contains the value 2, and cell A2 contains the value 5, you can write a formula that reads =A1+A2 in any cell and that new cell will contain the result of the calculation: 7.

ACTIVITY 3-1

Creating Basic Formulas

Objective:

To create basic formulas.

Data Files:

- Calculations

Setup:

Close any open files. Open the file Calculations.

Scenario:

The following figure, Figure 3-4, shows a worksheet you have designed that tracks sales data.

Books and Beyond - Northeastern Region								
5/15/2002								
					Commission Rate:		17%	
	Employee ID	January	February	March	April		YTD Total	YTD Average
	123456789	110.25	175.65	140.96	135.15			
	234567890	200.75	210.63	240.82	205.79			
	345678901	210.34	185.11	195.14	310.44			
	456789012	220.15	195.37	185.66	250.15			
	Monthly Totals							
	Monthly Average							

Figure 3-4: *A worksheet that tracks sales data.*

You are now ready to add some calculations to the worksheet. Your manager would like to see:

- Monthly totals for all employees.
- Monthly averages for all employees.

What You Do	How You Do It
1. Total the January column.	a. Select cell C12.

b. In the Formula Bar, **type =C7+C8+C9+C10**

c. **Press Enter** to populate cell C12 with the January total.

2. **What is the January total?**
    a) 766.76
    b) 741.49
    c) 762.58
    d) 901.53

3. **Total the February column.**

a. **Select cell D12.**

b. In the Formula Bar, **type =**

c. **Select cell D7, and then type +**

d. **Select cell D8, and then type +**

e. **Select cell D9, and then type +**

f. **Select cell D10, and then press Enter** to populate cell D12 with the February total.

	February	M
25	175.65	
'5	210.63	
34	185.11	
5	195.37	
19	766.76	

4. **Total the March and April columns.**

a. **Select cell E12.**

b. **Type =SUM(**

c. **Click and drag a selection marquee around cells E7, E8, E9, and E10** to add this range of cells to the formula.

f_x	=SUM(E7:E10			
B	SUM(**number1**, [number2], ...)		E	F
- **Northeastern Region**				
				Commission
byee ID	January	February	March	April
123456789	110.25	175.65	140.96	135.15
234567890	200.75	210.63	240.82	205.79
345678901	210.34	185.11	195.14	310.44
456789012	220.15	195.37	185.68	250.15
				4R x 1C
ily Totals	741.49	766.76	1(E7:E10	
ily Average				

d. **Type) and press Enter** to apply the calculation.

e. **Select cell E12, and then click and drag the fill handle to cell F12** to apply the sum calculation to cell F12.

.37	185.66	250.15
.76	762.58	901.53

5. **Average the January column.**

a. **Select cell C13.**

b. In the Formula Bar, **type =(C7+C8+C9+C10)/4**

c. **Press Enter** to populate cell C13 with the January average.

Monthly Totals	741.49
Monthly Average	185.3725

6. **Average the February column.**

   a. **Select cell D13.**

   b. In the Formula Bar, **type =(**

   c. **Select cell D7, and then type +**

   d. **Select cell D8, and then type +**

   e. **Select cell D9, and then type +**

   f. **Select cell D10,** and then, in the Formula Bar, **type)/4**

   g. **Press Enter** to populate cell D13 with the February average.

Monthly Totals	741.49	766.76
Monthly Average	185.3725	191.69

7. **Average the March and April columns, and then save your work.**

   a. To populate cells E13 and F13 with their respective monthly averages, **select cell D13, and then click and drag the fill handle to cell F13.**

Monthly Totals	741.49	766.76	762.58	901.53
Monthly Average	185.3725	191.69	190.645	225.3825

   b. On the Standard toolbar, **click the Save button** .

TOPIC B

Calculate with Functions

You have run calculations using basic formulas. Now, you would like to perform calculations without using formulas. In this topic, you will calculate with functions.

You have a worksheet that contains the sales figures for sales representatives for the month of January. You don't want to take the time to write a formula to calculate the total sales for each employee. Rather than write a formula, you decide to use a built-in Excel function to calculate the total sales. Functions help speed up the development of calculations because they contain built-in formulas that you don't have to write out by hand.

Functions

Definition:

A *function* is a built-in formula in Excel. Functions start with an equal sign (=) and generally have two components:

- The *function name* or an abbreviation of that name.

- The *arguments*, which are required data enclosed in parentheses.

Excel provides over 200 built-in functions. You can use a function by itself or in conjunction with other formulas or functions.

Example: Functions

The following figure, Figure 3-5, shows an example of a function. See Table 3-1 for common functions in Excel.

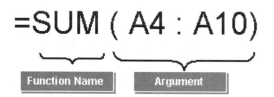

Figure 3-5: *An example of a function.*

Table 3-1: *Common Functions in Excel*

Functions	What It Does
=SUM(A4:A10)	Instructs Excel to add all values in cells A4 through A10.
=AVERAGE(A4:A10)	Instructs Excel to calculate the mean average of the values in cells A4 through A10.
=MIN(A4:A10)	Instructs Excel to find the minimum value of the values in cells A4 through A10.
=MAX(A4:A10)	Instructs Excel to find the maximum value of the values in cells A4 through A10.
=COUNT(A4:A10)	Instructs Excel to find the number of entries in cells A4 through A10.

How to Calculate with Functions

Procedure Reference: Calculate with Functions

To calculate with functions:

1. Select the cell in which you would like the function to appear.

2. If you are only going to sum a range of cells, click the AutoSum button. Otherwise, choose Insert→Function to open the Insert Function dialog box.

3. On the Select A Function list, double-click the function you would like to use.

4. On the worksheet, select the cells you want to include in the function.

5. In the Function Arguments dialog box, click OK to insert the function into the cell and populate the cell with the results of the function.

ACTIVITY 3-2

Calculating with Functions

Objective:

To calculate with functions.

Setup:

Activity 3-1 is complete. The file Calculations is open.

Scenario:

Your manager wants to add totals and averages at the year-to-date level for each employee ID on the sales data worksheet. Additionally, she wants to know, at a glance, the highest and lowest sales totals for each month. You've decided to use functions—rather than create basic formulas—to calculate these numbers, because functions will save you a considerable amount of time and help you get the worksheet back to your manager on schedule.

What You Do	How You Do It
1. Total the YTD total for the first Employee ID.	a. Select cell H7.
	b. Click the AutoSum button ⟨Σ⟩.

c. **Draw a selection marquee around cells C7, D7, E7, and F7.**

123456789	110.25	175.65	140.96	135.15
234567890	200.75	210.63	240.82	205.79
345678901	210.34	185.11	185.14	210.44

1R x 4C

d. **Press Enter** to populate cell H7 with the YTD total for Employee ID 123456789.

e. **Select cell H7, hover your mouse pointer over the warning icon** ⚠ **, and then read the tool tip** that indicates that the formula refers to a range of cells with additional numbers adjacent to it. In this case, this refers to the Employee ID field, which contains a number that you do not want to include in your calculation.

---

2. **Total the YTD totals for the remaining Employee IDs.**

a. **Select cell H8.**

b. **Choose Insert→Function** to open the Insert Function dialog box with the SUM function selected by default.

Insert Function

Search for a function:

> Type a brief description of what you want to do and then click Go   [Go]

Or select a category: Most Recently Used

Select a function:

> SUM
> AVERAGE
> IF
> HYPERLINK
> COUNT
> MAX
> SIN

SUM(number1,number2,...)
Adds all the numbers in a range of cells.

Help on this function   [OK]   [Cancel]

c. In the Select A Function region of the Insert Function dialog box, **double-click SUM** to open the Function Arguments dialog box.

Function Arguments		
SUM		
Number1 B8:G8		= {234567890,200.75
Number2		= number
		= 234568748

Adds all the numbers in a range of cells.

Number1: number1,number2,... are 1 to 30 numbers to sum. Logical values and text are ignored in cells, included if typed as arguments.

Formula result =   234568748

Help on this function   OK   Cancel

d. **Drag the Function Arguments dialog box so that you can see its contents and cells C8 through F8 in the worksheet.**

B	C	D	E	F
123456789	110.25	175.65	140.96	135.15
234567890	200.75	210.63	240.82	205.79

Function Arguments	
SUM	
Month	**Number1** B8:G8

e. On the worksheet, **drag a selection marquee around cells C8, D8, E8, and F8.** The Function Arguments dialog box will minimize while you do this.

123450789	110.25	175.65	140.96	135.15		562.01
234567890	200.75	210.63	240.82	205.79		IM(C8:F8)

Function Arguments   1R x 4C

C8:F8

nthly Totals	741.49	766.76	762.58	901.53
nthly Average	185.3725	191.69	190.645	225.3825

f. In the Function Arguments dialog box, **click OK** to populate cell H8 with the YTD total for Employee ID 234567890.

YTD Total	Y
562.01	
857.99	

g. **Drag the fill handle from cell H8 down to cell H10** to populate the YTD totals for the last two Employee IDs.

YTD Total
562.01
857.99
901.03
851.33

---

3. **Average the YTD average for the first Employee ID.**

a. **Select cell I7.**

b. **Click the drop-down arrow next to the AutoSum button.**

c. **Select Average.**

d. **Draw a selection marquee around cells C7, D7, E7, and F7, and then press Enter** to populate cell I7 with the YTD average for Employee ID 123456789.

---

4. **Average the YTD averages for the remaining Employee IDs.**

a. With cell I8 selected, **choose Insert→ Function** to open the Insert Function dialog box.

b. In the Select A Function region of the Insert Function dialog box, **double-click AVERAGE** to open the Function Arguments dialog box.

c. **Drag the Function Arguments dialog box so that you can see its contents and cells C8 through F8 in the worksheet.**

d. On the worksheet, **drag a selection marquee around cells C8, D8, E8, and F8.**

e. In the Function Arguments dialog box, **click OK** to populate cell I8 with the YTD average for Employee ID 234567890.

f. **Drag cell I8's fill handle down to cell I10** to populate the YTD averages for the last two Employee IDs.

5. **Create a row that displays the highest value for each month.**

a. **Select cell B15, type** *Highest* **and press Enter.**

Monthly Totals	
Monthly Average	1E
Highest	

b. **Select cell C15, and then click the drop-down arrow next to the AutoSum button.**

c. **Select Max, drag a selection marquee around cells C7, C8, C9, and C10, and press Enter.**

	January	F
9	110.25	
0	200.75	
1	210.34	
2	220.15	
	741.49	
e	185.3725	
	220.15	

d. **Select cell C15, and then drag the fill handle to cell F15** to populate cells D15 through F15 with the maximum value for each month.

Highest	220.15	210.63	240.82	310.44

6. **Create a row that displays the lowest value for each month, and then save your work.**

a. **Select cell B16, type** *Lowest* **and press Enter.**

b. **Select cell C16, and then choose Insert→Function to open the Insert Function dialog box.**

c. From the Or Select A Category drop-down list, **select Statistical.**

d. In the Select A Function region, **scroll to MIN, select it, and then click OK** to open the Function Arguments dialog box.

e. **Drag the Function Arguments dialog box so that you can see its contents and cells C7 through C10 in the worksheet.**

f. On the worksheet, **drag a selection marquee around cells C7, C8, C9, and C10.**

g. In the Function Arguments dialog box, **click OK** to populate cell C16 with the minimum value for the month of January.

h. **Drag cell C16's fill handle to cell F16 to** populate cells D16 through F16 with the minimum value for each month.

i. On the Standard toolbar, **click the Save button** 🖫 .

TOPIC C

Copy Formulas and Functions

You have calculated data using formulas and functions. Now you need to use the same formulas and functions in multiple cells. In this topic, you will copy formulas and functions.

You can copy formulas and functions just like you can copy text in a worksheet. By copying formulas and functions, you can reuse some of the formulas and functions in other cells, and your calculations will contain fewer errors because you aren't manually keying the formulas and functions.

How to Copy Formulas and Functions

Procedure Reference: Copy a Formula or Function to Maintain the Original Value

When you want to copy a formula or function from an originating cell to a destination cell, and you want the destination cell to contain the same value as the originating cell:

1. Select the cell that contains the formula you want to copy.

2. Select the contents of the Formula Bar.

3. Choose Edit→Copy, and then press Enter.

4. Select the cell that you want to copy the formula to.

5. Choose Edit→Paste.

Procedure Reference: Copy a Formula or Function to Create a New Value

When you want to copy a formula or function from an originating cell to a destination cell, and you want the destination cell to contain a new value relative to a new set of cells different from the originating cell:

1. Select the cell that contains the formula you want to copy.

2. Select the contents of the Formula Bar.

3. Choose Edit→Copy, and then press Enter.

4. Select the cell that you want to copy the formula to.

5. Choose Edit→Paste.

6. Double-click the cell(s) bounded by the selection marquee to activate the selection marquee.

7. Drag the handles of the selection marquee around the cells on which you want the formula or function to operate.

8. Press Enter to populate the cell with the calculated value.

Relative References

Definition:

A *relative reference* is a cell reference that is automatically updated by Excel whenever a formula or function is copied from an originating cell to a destination cell. Relative references include only a cell's column and row identification.

Example: A Relative Reference

You have a worksheet with two columns. You've already totalled the January column. Rather than write another function to total the February column, you choose to copy the function from the January column to the February column. When you do this, Excel automatically creates relative references for the cells in the February column.

ACTIVITY 3-3

Copying Formulas and Functions

Objective:

To copy formulas and functions.

Setup:

Activity 3-2 is complete. The file Calculations is open.

Scenario:

Your manager would now like to add a Totals Summary section to the sales data worksheet to help her quickly locate all of the totals in a single area. She has provided you with a printed copy of the existing worksheet with some notes. The following figure, Figure 3-6, shows the Sales Data worksheet with her comment.

	A	B	C	D	E	F	G	H	I
1	Books and Beyond - Northeastern Region								
2	5/15/2002								
3						Commission Rate:		17%	
4									
5		Employee ID	January	February	March	April		YTD Total	YTD Average
6									
7		123456789	110.25	175.65	140.96	135.15		562.01	140.5025
8		234567890	200.75	210.63	240.82	205.79		857.99	214.4975
9		345678901	210.34	185.11	195.14	310.44		901.03	225.2575
10		456789012	220.15	195.37	185.66	250.15		851.33	212.8325
11									
12		Monthly Totals	741.49	766.76	762.58	901.53			
13		Monthly Average	185.3725	191.69	190.645	225.3825			
14									
15		Highest	220.15	210.63	240.82	310.44			
16		Lowest	110.25	175.65	140.96	135.15			
17									

From your manager:

"I need a section here that summarizes each monthly total and the entire YTD total for all employees."

Figure 3-6: *The sales data worksheet.*

Because you have already created formulas and functions that do these calculations, you have decided to copy the needed formulas and functions to speed your development time.

What You Do	How You Do It
1. **Add the Totals Summary section headings.**	a. In cell B19, type *Totals Summary* and press Enter.

18	
19	Totals Summary
20	

b. Select cell B21, type *January* and press Enter.

c. Type *February* and press Enter.

d. Type *March* and press Enter.

e. Type *April* and press Enter.

f. **Select cell B26, type *YTD* and press Enter.**

```
Totals Summary

January
February
March
April

YTD

```

2. **Copy the monthly total formulas to the new Totals Summary section.**

a. **Select cell C12, and then drag to select the contents of the Formula Bar.**

```
fx =C7+C8+C9+C10
   B          C
```

b. **Choose Edit→Copy, and then press Enter to deselect the contents of the Formula Bar.**

c. **Select cell C21, and then choose Edit→ Paste to paste the formula into the destination cell.**

```
Totals Summary

January           741.49
```

d. **Select cell D12, and then drag to select the contents of the Formula Bar.**

e. **Choose Edit→Copy, and then press Enter to deselect the contents of the Formula Bar.**

f. **Select cell C22, and then choose Edit→ Paste** to paste the formula into the destination cell.

Totals Summary	
January	741.49
February	766.76

---

3. **Copy the March and April monthly total formulas to the new Totals Summary section.**

a. **Select cell E12, and then drag to select the contents of the Formula Bar.**

b. **Choose Edit→Copy, and then press Enter** to deselect the contents of the Formula Bar.

c. **Select cell C23, and then choose Edit→ Paste** to paste the formula into the destination cell.

d. **Select cell F12, and then drag to select the contents of the Formula Bar.**

e. **Choose Edit→Copy, and then press Enter** to deselect the contents of the Formula Bar.

    🖈 If necessary, close the Clipboard task pane.

f. **Select cell C24, and then choose Edit→ Paste** to paste the formula into the destination cell.

Totals Summary	
January	741.49
February	766.76
March	762.58
April	901.53

---

4. **Copy one of the existing formulas or functions that sums a range, use it to total the YTD total in the Totals Summary region, and then save your work.**

a. **Select cell H7, and then drag to select the contents of the Formula Bar.**

b. **Choose Edit→Copy, and then press Enter** to deselect the contents of the Formula Bar.

c. **Select cell C26, and then choose Edit→
    Paste** to paste the formula into the
    destination cell.

| YTD | ◇ | 562.01 |

d. **Double-click cell C26** to activate the
    selection marquee around cells C7 through
    F7.

	C	D	E	F
				Commission
	January	February	March	April
39	110.25	175.65	140.96	135.15
30	200.75	210.63	240.82	205.79

e. **Drag the bottom-right corner of the
    selection marquee to cell H10.**

M(Or. r r ru)

	C	D	E	F	G	H	
					Commission Rate:	17%	
	January	February	March	April		YTD Total	Y
39	110.25	175.65	140.96	135.15		562.01	
30	200.75	210.63	240.82	205.79		857.99	
31	210.34	185.11	195.14	310.44		901.03	
12	220.15	195.37	185.66	250.15		851.33	

f. **Drag the top-left corner of the selection
    marquee to cell H7.**

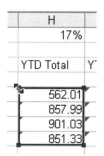

H	
17%	
YTD Total	Y
562.01	
857.99	
901.03	
851.33	

g. **Press Enter** to populate the cell with the new value.

YTD	3172.36

h. On the Standard toolbar, **click the Save button** 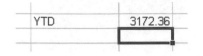 .

TOPIC D

Create an Absolute Reference

You have run calculations on data. You now have a formula that needs to reference the data stored in another cell. In this topic, you will create an absolute reference.

You have a cell labeled "Commissions" that stores the percentage your sales reps earn on their sales. The worksheet also contains many formulas that use the commission value to determine payment to the sales reps. By identifying the Commissions cell as an absolute reference, you will only have to change the commission rate in one place (the Commissions cell) rather than in multiple places (each formula) as the commission rate changes.

Absolute References

Definition:

An *absolute reference* is a cell reference in a formula that doesn't change when you copy the formula. All absolute references include dollar signs ($) either before both the column and row headings or before either the column or row headings.

Example: An Absolute Reference

You can convert any relative cell reference to an absolute reference by adding a dollar sign in front of the cell's column and row headings.

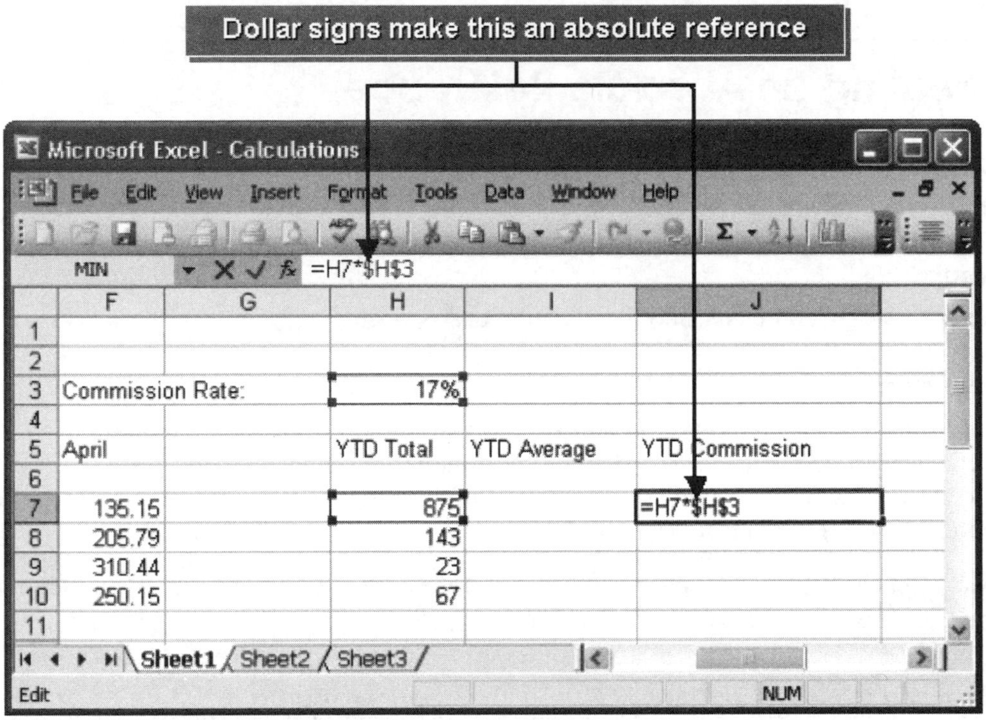

Figure 3-7: *An absolute reference.*

How to Create an Absolute Reference

Procedure Reference: Create an Absolute Reference

To create an absolute reference:

1. Select the cell that contains the formula you want to add the absolute reference to.

2. Type a dollar sign ($) in front of the column heading and row heading for each column and row you want to refer to absolutely. For example, to create an absolute reference to cell B3, in a formula, you would change B3 to B3.

3. Press Enter to activate the absolute reference(s).

ACTIVITY 3-4

Creating an Absolute Reference

Objective:

To create an absolute reference.

Setup:

Activity 3-3 is complete. The file Calculations is open.

Scenario:

Your manager has asked you to add a YTD Commissions heading and column to the sales data worksheet to help her quickly identify the total commissions earned by each employee. She wants the new YTD Commissions section and heading to appear immediately to the right of the existing YTD Average section.

You want the formula for each employee to reference the Commission Rate value, and you want to reuse one formula for each employee.

What You Do	How You Do It
1. Add the *YTD Commissions* section heading, and then calculate the YTD commission for the first employee.	a. Select cell J5, type *YTD Commission* and press Enter.

J
YTD Commission

b. Select cell J7, type = and select cell H7 to begin the formula in the Formula Bar.

YTD Total	YTD Average	YTD Commission
562.01	140.5025	=H7
857.99	214.4975	

c. **Type *, select cell H3, and then press
    Enter** to add the YTD commission value to
    the cell.

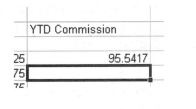

---

2. **Create an absolute reference to the
    commission rate, copy the formula
    to the remaining employees, and
    then save your work. Then, close
    the file.**

a. **Select cell J7, and in the Formula Bar,
    drag to select the H3 value.**

b. **Type _H3_** to convert the relative refer-
    ence to an absolute reference.

c. **Press Enter.**

d. **Select cell J7, and then drag the fill
    handle to cell J10** to populate the
    remaining cells with their corresponding
    YTD commissions.

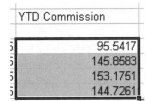

e. On the Standard toolbar, **click the Save
    button.**

f. **Close the file.**

Lesson 3 Follow-up

In this lesson, you performed calculations on existing data. By using Excel to perform calculations on your data, you remove the inefficiency of calculating by hand.

1.   **What data are you currently working with that you could enter into an Excel spreadsheet and run calculations on?**

2.   **What kind of calculations might you run on that data?**

LESSON 4
Formatting a Worksheet

Lesson Time
1 hour(s), 30 minutes

Lesson Objectives:

In this lesson, you will format a worksheet.

You will:

- Change font size and type.
- Add borders and color to cells.
- Change column width and row height.
- Merge cells.
- Apply number formats to cells.
- Create a custom number format.
- Align cell contents.
- Find and replace formats.
- Apply an AutoFormat.
- Apply styles.

Introduction

You've created a basic worksheet that includes raw data and calculations. You want to define specific areas of your worksheet to make it easier to visually locate data. You can do this by formatting your worksheet.

Of the two following spreadsheets, which spreadsheet makes it easier to differentiate between sales reps?

	A	B	C	D	E	F	G	H
2				U.S. Sales 2003				
3								
4	Last Name	First Name	Region	Qtr 1	Qtr 2	Qtr 3	Qtr 4	Total
5	Arman	Simon	East	$ 14,815.00	$ 13,100.00	$ 11,580.00	$ 17,300.00	$ 56,795.00
6	Bartholomew	Barbara	North	$ 24,500.00	$ 25,600.00	$ 22,000.00	$ 19,000.00	$ 91,100.00
7	Childs	Alice	West	$ 20,900.00	$ 22,600.00	$ 20,140.00	$ 24,400.00	$ 88,040.00
8	Greenburg	Linda	East	$ 15,900.00	$ 22,700.00	$ 17,600.00	$ 20,000.00	$ 76,200.00
9	Lundquist	Sam	North	$ 25,000.00	$ 34,000.00	$ 21,000.00	$ 35,000.00	$ 115,000.00
10	McTague	Michael	Northwest	$ 24,110.00	$ 54,812.00	$ 15,200.00	$ 25,600.00	$ 119,722.00
11	Quayle	Antonio	West	$ 25,600.00	$ 48,752.00	$ 30,300.00	$ 22,600.00	$ 127,252.00
12	Rivena	Orlando	South	$ 22,600.00	$ 58,445.00	$ 16,800.00	$ 22,700.00	$ 120,545.00
13	Stark	Oscar	Southwest	$ 22,700.00	$ 48,648.00	$ 36,855.00	$ 35,000.00	$ 143,203.00
14	Unger	Maria	Southwest	$ 23,300.00	$ 24,600.00	$ 21,380.00	$ 15,937.00	$ 85,217.00

Figure 4-1: *An unformatted worksheet.*

	A	B	C	D	E	F	G	H
2				U.S. Sales 2003				
3								
4	Last Name	First Name	Region	Qtr 1	Qtr 2	Qtr 3	Qtr 4	Total
5	Arman	Simon	East	$ 14,815.00	$ 13,100.00	$ 11,580.00	$ 17,300.00	$ 56,795.00
6	Bartholomew	Barbara	North	$ 24,500.00	$ 25,600.00	$ 22,000.00	$ 19,000.00	$ 91,100.00
7	Childs	Alice	West	$ 20,900.00	$ 22,600.00	$ 20,140.00	$ 24,400.00	$ 88,040.00
8	Greenburg	Linda	East	$ 15,900.00	$ 22,700.00	$ 17,600.00	$ 20,000.00	$ 76,200.00
9	Lundquist	Sam	North	$ 25,000.00	$ 34,000.00	$ 21,000.00	$ 35,000.00	$ 115,000.00
10	McTague	Michael	Northwest	$ 24,110.00	$ 54,812.00	$ 15,200.00	$ 25,600.00	$ 119,722.00
11	Quayle	Antonio	West	$ 25,600.00	$ 48,752.00	$ 30,300.00	$ 22,600.00	$ 127,252.00
12	Rivena	Orlando	South	$ 22,600.00	$ 58,445.00	$ 16,800.00	$ 22,700.00	$ 120,545.00
13	Stark	Oscar	Southwest	$ 22,700.00	$ 48,648.00	$ 36,855.00	$ 35,000.00	$ 143,203.00
14	Unger	Maria	Southwest	$ 23,300.00	$ 24,600.00	$ 21,380.00	$ 15,937.00	$ 85,217.00
15	Hanover	Caroline	East	$ 23,800.00	$ 27,700.00	$ 12,600.00	$ 35,000.00	$ 99,100.00
16	Jaen	Enrique	West	$ 54,826.00	$ 598,224.00	$ 24,100.00	$ 28,000.00	$ 705,150.00
17	Monder	Alana	Southwest	$ 31,200.00	$ 23,100.00	$ 17,700.00	$ 29,300.00	$ 101,300.00
18	Innoue	Chika	South	$ 50,224.00	$ 17,300.00	$ 15,200.00	$ 14,600.00	$ 97,324.00

Figure 4-2: *A formatted worksheet.*

Formatting can visually differentiate one set of data from other sets, making it easier to quickly locate information.

TOPIC A

Change Font Size and Type

You are familiar with the Excel environment and how to enter, edit, and manipulate the data in a worksheet. Now you want to make it easier to visually locate data in a worksheet. One way to do this is by changing the font size and type for specific pieces of data.

Which of the following worksheets is easier to read, the one shown in Figure 4-3 or the one shown in Figure 4-4?

	A	B	C	D	E	F	G	H
1	*Books and Beyond – Northeastern Region*							
2	5/15/2003							
3						Commission Rate:		17%
4								
5		Employee ID	January	February	March	April		YTD Average
6								
7		123456789	110.25	175.65	140.96	135.15		140.50
8		234567890	200.75	210.63	240.82	205.79		214.50
9		345678901	210.34	185.11	195.14	310.44		225.26
10		456789012	220.15	195.37	185.66	250.15		212.83
11								
12		Monthly Totals						
13		Monthly Average						
14								

Figure 4-3: *A worksheet with difficult to read text.*

	A	B	C	D	E	F	G	H
1	**Books and Beyond - Northeastern Region**							
2	5/15/2003							
3						Commission Rate:		17%
4								
5		Employee ID	January	February	March	April		YTD Average
6								
7		123456789	110.25	175.65	140.96	135.15		140.50
8		234567890	200.75	210.63	240.82	205.79		214.50
9		345678901	210.34	185.11	195.14	310.44		225.26
10		456789012	220.15	195.37	185.66	250.15		212.83
11								
12		Monthly Totals						
13		Monthly Average						

Figure 4-4: *A worksheet with data in a readable font.*

By changing the font size and type, you can change the appearance of your data to make it easier to read and easier to locate critical information.

Fonts

Definition:

A *font* is a complete set of type characters comprised of the same:

- Typeface (such as Times New Roman or Arial). The typeface is the style or design of a set of characters.
- Size (such as 12 point). Font size is measured in points, and one point equals 1/72 of an inch.

Example: Fonts

Some common fonts are shown in Figure 4-5.

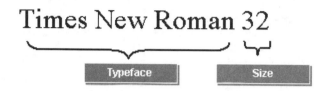

Arial 12
Arial 20
Times New Roman 14
Times New Roman 32
Typeface
Size

Figure 4-5: *Some examples of fonts.*

How to Change Font Size and Type

Procedure Reference: Change Font Type

To change the font type:

1. Select the cell(s) that contain(s) the font you want to change.
2. From the Font drop-down list, select the new font face to change the font.

Procedure Reference: Change Font Size

To change the font size:

1. Select the cell(s) that contain(s) the font you want to change.
2. From the Font Size drop-down list, select the new font size to change the size of the font.

ACTIVITY 4-1

Changing Font Size and Type

Objective:

To change the size and type of fonts.

Setup:

Excel is running. The file Calculations is open.

Scenario:

You have recommended to your manager that you can make the sales data worksheet easier to read by applying different formatting techniques to it. She has agreed with you and likes your ideas. You will first change the font size and type of all of the headings on the worksheet. Because your company uses Verdana as its primary font in other publications, you are going to convert the entire worksheet to this font.

What You Do	How You Do It
1. Convert the entire worksheet to Verdana.	a. **Click the blank box immediately below the Name Box** to select the entire worksheet.
	b. From the Font drop-down list, **select Verdana** to convert the entire worksheet to the new font.
2. Convert the main heading to size 16 font.	a. **Select cell A1.**
	b. From the Font Size drop-down list, **select 16.**

3. Change the Commission Rate, Monthly Totals, Monthly Average, Highest, and Lowest headings to size 12 font.

   a. Select cell F3, press and hold Ctrl, and then click cells B12, B13, B15, and B16 to select the contents of each of these cells.

	A	B	C	D	E	F	G
1	**Books and Beyond – Northeastern Region**						
2	5/15/2002						
3						Commission Rate:	
4							
5		Employee ID	January	February	March	April	
6							
7		123456789	110.25	175.65	140.96	135.15	
8		234567890	200.75	210.63	240.82	205.79	
9		345678901	210.34	185.11	195.14	310.44	
10		456789012	220.15	195.37	185.66	250.15	
11							
12		Monthly Totals	741.49	766.76	762.58	901.53	
13		Monthly Averag	185.373	191.69	190.645	225.383	
14							
15		Highest	220.15	210.63	240.82	310.44	
16		Lowest	110.25				
17							

   b. From the Font Size drop-down list, **select 12** to change the size of the selected headings. Some of the headings will no longer fit properly in their cells. You will fix this at another time.

Monthly Tot	741.
Monthly Ave	185.3
Highest	220.
Lowest	110.

4. Change the Employee ID, months, YTD, and Totals Summary headings to size 12 font.

   a. Click the row 5 row heading, press and hold Ctrl, and then click the row 19 row heading to select both rows.

   b. From the Font Size drop-down list, **select 12** to change the size of the selected headings. Some of the headings will no longer fit properly in their cells. You will fix this at another time.

Employee IE	Januar	Februar	March	April

   c. On the Standard toolbar, **click the Save button.**

TOPIC B

Add Borders and Color to Cells

You have changed the font size and type for data. Another way to make it easier to visually locate data is to highlight cells. In this topic, you will add borders and color to cells.

Which worksheet makes it easier to locate the Totals cells, the worksheet in Figure 4-6 or the worksheet in Figure 4-7?

	A	B	C	D	E	F	G	H	I
1	Books and Beyond - Northeastern Region								
2	5/15/2002								
3						Commission Rate:		17%	
4									
5		Employee ID	January	February	March	April		YTD Total	YTD Average
6									
7		123456789	110.25	175.65	140.96	135.15		562.01	140.50
8		234567890	200.75	210.63	240.82	205.79		857.99	214.50
9		345678901	210.34	185.11	195.14	310.44		901.03	225.26
10		456789012	220.15	195.37	185.66	250.15		851.33	212.83
11									
12		Monthly Totals	741.49	766.76	762.58	901.53			
13		Monthly Average	185.37	191.69	190.65	225.38			
14									
15		Overall Yearly Total		3172.36					
16		Overall Yearly Average		198.27					

Figure 4-6: *A worksheet with no cell borders or colors.*

	A	B	C	D	E	F	G	H	I
1	Books and Beyond - Northeastern Region								
2	5/15/2002								
3						Commission Rate:		17%	
4									
5		Employee ID	January	February	March	April		YTD Total	YTD Average
6									
7		123456789	110.25	175.65	140.96	135.15		562.01	140.50
8		234567890	200.75	210.63	240.82	205.79		857.99	214.50
9		345678901	210.34	185.11	195.14	310.44		901.03	225.26
10		456789012	220.15	195.37	185.66	250.15		851.33	212.83
11									
12		Monthly Totals	741.49	766.76	762.58	901.53			
13		Monthly Average	185.37	191.69	190.65	225.38			
14									
15		Overall Yearly Total		3172.36					
16		Overall Yearly Average		198.27					
17									

Figure 4-7: *A worksheet with cell borders and colors.*

Adding borders and colors to cells helps you quickly locate critical information.

Border Options

You can apply a border to some or all of the sides of a cell or range of cells and determine the borderline style and color. The following figure, Figure 4-8, shows a tab in the Format Cells dialog box.

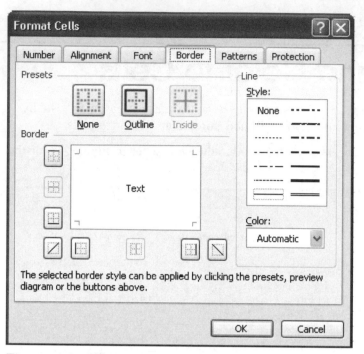

Figure 4-8: *The Border tab of the Format Cells dialog box.*

Background Options

You can apply a background to an entire worksheet. A background can be a graphic, such as a line drawing or photograph.

How to Add Borders and Color to Cells

Procedure Reference: Add Borders to Cells

To add borders to cells:

1. Select the cell(s) that you would like to add a border to.

2. Either click the Borders button or choose Format→Cells to open the Format Cells dialog box. If using the Format Cells dialog box, continue with this procedure; otherwise stop.

3. Click the Border tab to view the border options.

4. From the Style list, select the border style.

5. Use either the preset border buttons or the specific border buttons to set the borders for the selected cell(s).

6. Click OK to apply the borders.

Procedure Reference: Add Colors to Cells

To add colors to cells:

1. Select the cell(s) that you would like to add a color to.

2. Either click the Fill Color button or choose Format→Cells to open the Format Cells dialog box. If using the Format Cells dialog box, continue with this procedure; otherwise stop.

3. Click the Patterns tab to view the pattern options.

4. In the Cell Shading region, select the fill color.

5. Click OK to apply the color.

Procedure Reference: Add a Background to a Worksheet

To add a background to a worksheet:

1. Select the worksheet that you would like to add the background to.

2. Choose Format→Sheet→Background to open the Sheet Background dialog box.

3. Navigate to your background of choice and then double-click it to apply the background to the worksheet.

Paste Special

The Paste Special command allows you to specify how you would like the contents of the clipboard pasted into Excel. The Paste Special dialog box provides you with the available options, as shown in Figure 4-9.

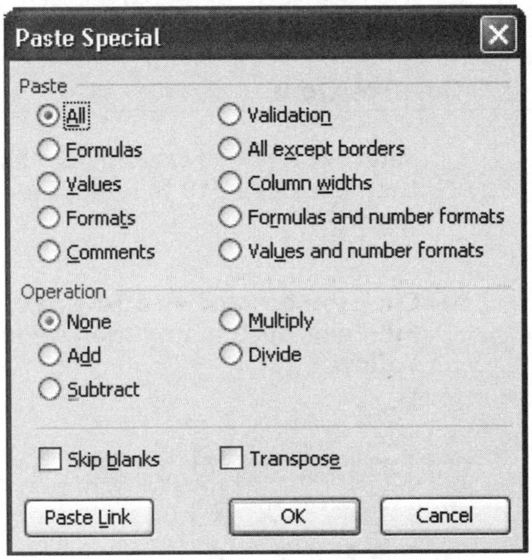

Figure 4-9: *The Paste Special dialog box.*

ACTIVITY 4-2

Adding Borders and Colors to Cells

Objective:

To add borders and colors to cells.

Setup:

Activity 4-1 is complete. The file Calculations is open.

Scenario:

The formatting of your sales data worksheet is coming along nicely. You are now ready to add borders and colors to some of the cells to help draw attention to specific regions of the worksheet. Your manager would like to see a box around the Totals Summary and YTD regions of the worksheet. She would also like these regions to be highlighted with a bright color. Additionally, you apply a background to the entire worksheet, but, after assessing the background, decide that it is not appropriate for the data. You then remove the background.

What You Do	How You Do It
1. **Add a bright colored background to the YTD region.**	a. **Select cell H5, press and hold Shift, and then click cell J10** to select the YTD region.
	b. **Click the drop-down arrow next to the Fill Color button, and then select Yellow.**

c. **Click any cell outside of the selected region** to deselect the region so you can see the fill color.

YTD Total	YTD Average	YTD Commission
562.01	140.5025	95.5417
857.99	214.4975	145.8583
901.03	225.2575	153.1751
851.33	212.8325	144.7261

2. **Add a bright colored background to the Totals Summary region.**

a. **Select cell H5, press and hold Shift, and then click cell J10 to select the YTD region.**

b. **Choose Edit→Copy.**

c. **Select cell B19, press and hold Shift, and then click cell C26 to select the Totals Summary region.**

d. **Choose Edit→Paste Special** to open the Paste Special dialog box.

e. Under Paste, **select Formats, and then click OK** to apply the yellow formatting to the Totals Summary region.

3. **Add a border around the Totals Summary region of the worksheet.**

a. With the Totals Summary region selected, choose **Format→Cells** to open the Format Cells dialog box.

b. **Click the Border tab** to view the Border options.

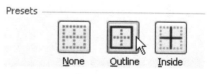

c. In the Line region, from the Style list, **click the thickest solid single line.**

d. In the Presets region, **click the Outline button.**

e. In the Format Cells dialog box, **click OK** to apply border.

f. **Click any cell outside of the selected region** to deselect the region so you can see the border.

Totals Summary	
January	741.49
February	766.76
March	762.58
April	901.53
YTD	3172.36

4. **Add a border around the YTD region of the worksheet.**

a. **Select cell H5, press and hold Shift, and then click cell J10 to select the YTD region.**

b. **Click the drop-down arrow next to the Borders button, and then select Thick Box Border.**

c. **Click any cell outside of the selected region to deselect the region so you can see the border.**

YTD Tota	YTD Averag	YTD Commission
562.01	140.5025	95.5417
857.99	214.4975	145.8583
901.03	225.2575	153.1751
851.33	212.8325	144.7261

5. **Add a background to the entire worksheet, and then remove the background and save your work.**

    a. **Choose Format→Sheet→Background** to open the Sheet Background dialog box.

    📌 If you are using Windows 2000, double-click the Sample icon, and then continue with step 5d.

    b. **Double-click the Sample Pictures icon.**

    c. **Double-click the Blue Hills file name** to apply the background to the entire worksheet.

    d. The background is too dark for this worksheet, so you will remove it. **Choose Format→Sheet→Delete Background.**

    e. On the Standard toolbar, **click the Save button.**

TOPIC C

Change Column Width and Row Height

You have changed the formatting of fonts and cells. Now, you need to alter the width of columns and the height of rows so that the data stored in the columns and rows fits in their respective cells. In this topic, you will change the width of columns and the height of rows.

You have some data that does not display correctly, as shown in Figure 4-10. By changing the column width and row height, your data will display as you intended it to, as shown in Figure 4-11.

	A	B	C	D	E	F	G	H	I	
1	Books and Beyond - Northeastern Region									
2	5/15/2002									
3						Commission R		17%		
4										
5		Employ	Jan	Febr	March		April	YTD Total	YTD Average	
6										
7		1E+08	##	176	140.96	#		562.01	140.50	
8		2E+08	##	211	240.82	#		857.99	214.50	
9		3E+08	##	185	195.14	#		901.03	225.26	
10		5E+08	##	195	185.66	#		851.33	212.83	
11										
12		Monthly	##	767	762.58	#				
13		Monthly	##	###	190.65	#				
14										
15		Overall Yea	###							
16		Overall Yea	###							
17										
18										
19										

Figure 4-10: *A worksheet with narrow columns.*

	A	B	C	D	E	F	G	H	I
1	Books and Beyond - Northeastern Region								
2	5/15/2002								
3						Commission Rate:		17%	
4									
5		Employee ID	January	February	March	April		YTD Total	YTD Average
6									
7		123456789	110.25	175.65	140.96	135.15		562.01	140.50
8		234567890	200.75	210.63	240.82	205.79		857.99	214.50
9		345678901	210.34	185.11	195.14	310.44		901.03	225.26
10		456789012	220.15	195.37	185.66	250.15		851.33	212.83
11									
12		Monthly Totals	741.49	766.76	762.58	901.53			
13		Monthly Average	185.37	191.69	190.65	225.38			
14									
15		Overall Yearly Total		3172.36					
16		Overall Yearly Average		198.27					
17									
18									

Figure 4-11: *A worksheet with columns that are wide enough to properly display their data.*

How to Change Column Width and Row Height

Procedure Reference: Change Column Width by Dragging Column Boundaries

To change column width:

1. In the column heading row, point the mouse pointer at the boundary between the column you want to change and its adjacent column.

2. Drag to the left or right to adjust the column width as needed.

Procedure Reference: Change Column Width by Selecting the Column

To change column width:

1. Select the column you want to change.

2. Choose Format→Column→Width to open the Column Width dialog box.

3. In the Column Width field, enter a new value for the column width.

4. Click OK to change the column width.

Procedure Reference: Change Row Height

To change row height:

1. Select the row you want to change.

2. Choose Format→Row→Height to open the Row Height dialog box.

3. In the Row Height field, enter a new value for the row height.

4. Click OK to change the row height.

Hide and Unhide

The Hide command allows you to hide any columns or rows in a worksheet. The columns and rows still exist in the worksheet, but are not visible to the user unless they are unhidden. The Unhide command is used to make visible any columns or rows you have previously hidden.

ACTIVITY 4-3

Changing Column Width and Row Height

Objective:

To change the column width and row height of selected columns and rows.

Setup:

Activity 4-2 is complete. The file Calculations is open.

Scenario:

While applying some of the other formatting techniques to the sales data worksheet, you noticed that some of the contents of a few of the columns extended beyond the right edge of the column and that the main heading looks cramped in its cell. You are now ready to adjust the column width of these columns so that the data fits correctly within its cells. You have also decided to increase the row height of the first row so that the main heading doesn't look cramped inside of its cell.

What You Do	How You Do It
1. **Widen the column that contains the Monthly Totals and Monthly Average headings so these headings fit within their respective cells, and then hide this column.**	a. **Point the mouse pointer at the boundary between the column B and column C headings** so that the mouse pointer will change to right and left pointing arrows.
	b. **Drag to the right until both the Monthly Totals and Monthly Average headings fit within their cells.**
	c. **Click the column B heading** to select the entire column.
	d. **Choose Format→Column→Hide** to hide column B while you work in other areas of the worksheet.
2. **Widen the columns for each month that currently doesn't fit within its cell.**	a. **Drag the boundary between the column C and column D headings until the January heading fits within its cell.**

b. **Drag the boundary between the column D and column E headings until the February heading fits within its cell.**

January	February	March	April

LESSON 4

3. **Widen the columns in the YTD region so each heading fits within its cell.**

   a. **Click the column H heading, press and hold Shift, and then click the column J heading.**

   b. **Choose Format→Column→Width** to open the Column Width dialog box.

   c. In the Column Width text box, **type 20**

   d. **Click OK** to apply the new width to the columns.

   e. **Click in any non-selected cell** to deselect the columns.

4. **Widen the row for the main heading, hide that row, and then save your work.**

   a. **Click the row 1 row heading** to select the row.

   b. **Choose Format→Row→Height** to open the Row Height dialog box.

c.   In the Row Height text box, **type** *30*

d.   **Click OK** to apply the new height to the row.

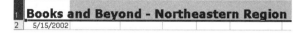

e.   **Choose Format→Row→Hide** to hide this row.

f.   **Click the Save button.**

TOPIC D

Merge Cells

You formatted cells by changing their height and width and by adding borders and colors to them. You now have a situation where you need to consolidate into a single cell data that stretches across multiple cells. In this topic, you will merge cells.

The title of your worksheet is contained in one cell, but the text is so long that it spreads across a number of cells, as shown in Figure 4-12. You can merge cells to improve the appearance of your worksheet, as shown in Figure 4-13.

	A	B	C	D
1	Books and Beyond - Northeastern Region			
2	5/15/2002			
3				
4				
5		Employee ID	January	February
6				
7		123456789	110.25	175.65

Figure 4-12: *A block of cells that have not been merged.*

	A	B	C
1	Books and Beyond - Northeastern Region		
2	5/15/2002		
3			

Figure 4-13: *The same block of cells merged into a single cell.*

Merge

The following figures, Figure 4-14 and Figure 4-15, show how you can select a contiguous range of cells and combine—or merge—them to create a single, large cell.

	A	B	C	D	E	
1						
2						
3						
4						
5						
6						
7						
8						
9						
10						
11						
12						

Figure 4-14: *Cells B2 through E5 before being merged.*

	A	B	C	D	E	F
1						
2						
3						
4						
5						
6						
7						
8						

Figure 4-15: *Cells B2 through E5 after being merged.*

How to Merge Cells

Procedure Reference: Merge Cells

To merge cells:

1. Select the range of contiguous cells you want to merge.

2. If you know you want to merge and center the contents of the selected cells, click the Merge And Center button. Otherwise, select Format→Cells to open the Format Cells dialog box.

3. On the Alignment tab, check the Merge Cells check box.

4. Click OK to merge the cells.

ACTIVITY 4-4

Merging Cells

Objective:

To merge cells.

Setup:

Activity 4-3 is complete. The file Calculations is open.

Scenario:

You are still formatting the sales data worksheet. You've noticed that you can only select the contents of the Books and Beyond heading when you click cell A1. You've also noticed that this heading actually spans across six separate cells—A1 through F1. To make the heading easier to manage, you've decided to merge the cells that it covers so the heading lives in a single, very wide cell. Additionally, you want the Totals Summary heading to live in a single cell that spans across the months and totals columns it appears above.

What You Do	How You Do It
1. Unhide column B and row 1.	a. **Click the blank box immediately below the Name Box** to select the entire worksheet.
	b. **Choose Format→Column→Unhide** to unhide column B.
	c. **Choose Format→Row→Unhide** to unhide row 1.
2. Merge the cells of the Books and Beyond heading into a single cell.	a. **Select cell A1, press and hold Shift, and then click cell F1** to select these cells.
	b. **Choose Format→Cells** to open the Format Cells dialog box.
	c. **Click the Alignment tab** to view the alignment options.

d. In the Text Control region, **check the Merge Cells check box.**

Text control
☐ Wrap text
☐ Shrink to fit
☑ Merge cells

e. **Click OK** to apply the merge.

3. **Merge the cells of the Totals Summary heading into a single cell, and then save your work.**

a. **Select cell B19, press and hold Shift, and then click cell C19** to select these cells.

b. On the Formatting toolbar, **click the Merge And Center button** to merge and center the cells.

c. **Click in any other cell** to deselect the Totals Summary heading.

d. **Click the Save button.**

TOPIC E

Apply Number Formats

You have learned basic formatting of data in a worksheet. You have additional options when formatting numeric data. In this topic, you will apply number formats.

Which worksheet, the one shown in Figure 4-16 or the one shown in Figure 4-17, makes it easier to interpret the values as currency?

Employee ID	January	February	March	April
123456789	110.25	175.65	140.96	135.15
234567890	200.75	210.63	240.82	205.79
345678901	210.34	185.11	195.14	310.44
456789012	220.15	195.37	185.66	250.15

Figure 4-16: *A worksheet with no number formats.*

Employee ID	January	February	March	April
123456789	$110.25	$175.65	$140.96	$135.15
234567890	$200.75	$210.63	$240.82	$205.79
345678901	$210.34	$185.11	$195.14	$310.44
456789012	$220.15	$195.37	$185.66	$250.15

Figure 4-17: *A worksheet with number formats applied.*

Applying number formats provides context to numeric data, making it easier to identify the type of data within cells.

Number Formats

Definition:

A number format is a format that forces the numerical data in a cell to display in a particular layout. You can apply a number format to a cell or a range of cells before or after you type in the numerical data. Excel's pre-installed number formats come in a variety of styles, including:

- Currency

- Accounting

- Date

- Time

- Percentage

- Fraction

- Scientific

Example: Number Formats

How to Apply Number Formats

Procedure Reference: Apply Number Formats

To apply a number format:

1. Select the cell(s) to which you want to apply the number format.

2. Choose Format→Cells to open the Format Cells dialog box.

3. Click the Number tab.

4. From the Category list, select the type of number format you want to apply.

5. Under Sample, make selections to specify the format layout.

6. Click OK to apply the format.

ACTIVITY 4-5

Applying Number Formats

Objective:

To apply number formats.

Setup:

Activity 4-4 is complete. The file Calculations is open.

Scenario:

Your manager has looked at your progress on the sales data worksheet and is very pleased. However, she would now like you to make some additional changes to it. She wants every monetary value to have no more than two decimal places and to appear with a dollar sign in US dollars (USD). Any negative number should appear in parentheses and be red in color. She also wants the date to appear like this: "15-May-02." This will help make the data easier to grasp for anyone else who might have to study the worksheet's data.

What You Do	How You Do It
1. Change the format of the numerical values for the months, monthly totals and averages, and highest and lowest regions, so they appear in USD.	a. Select cell **C7**, press and hold **Shift, and then click cell F16** to select these cells.
	b. Choose **Format→Cells** to open the Format Cells dialog box.
	c. **Click the Number tab** to view the number format options.

d. From the Category list, **select Currency.**

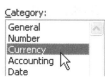

Category:

General
Number
Currency
Accounting
Date

e. From the Negative Numbers list, **select the red ($1234.10)** to force negative numbers to appear in red and be bounded by parentheses.

f. **Click OK** to apply the formatting.

$110.25	$175.65	#####	#####
$200.75	$210.63	#####	#####
$210.34	$185.11	#####	#####
$220.15	$195.37	#####	#####
$741.49	$766.76	#####	#####
$185.37	$191.69	#####	#####
$220.15	$210.63	#####	#####
$110.25	$175.65	#####	#####

g. **Point the mouse pointer at the boundary between the column E and column F headings, and then drag to the right until the March values fit within their cells.**

h. **Point the mouse pointer at the boundary between the column F and column G headings, and then drag to the right until the April values fit within their cells.**

$110.25	$175.65	$140.96	$135.15
$200.75	$210.63	$240.82	$205.79
$210.34	$185.11	$195.14	$310.44
$220.15	$195.37	$185.66	$250.15
$741.49	$766.76	$762.58	$901.53
$185.37	$191.69	$190.65	$225.38
$220.15	$210.63	$240.82	$310.44
$110.25	$175.65	$140.96	$135.15

LESSON 4

2. **Change the format of the numerical values for the Totals Summary region so they appear in USD.**

   a. **Select cell C21, press and hold Shift, and then click cell C26** to select these cells.

   b. **Right-click, and then choose Format Cells** to open the Format Cells dialog box.

✂	Cut
📋	Copy
📋	Paste
	Paste Special...
	Insert...
	Delete...
	Clear Contents
📋	Insert Comment
📋	Format Cells...
	Pick From Drop-down List...
	Create List...
🔍	Hyperlink...
🔍	Look Up...

   c. From the Category list, **select Currency.**

   d. From the Negative Numbers list, **select the red ($1234.10)** to force negative numbers to appear bounded by parentheses.

   e. **Click OK** to apply the formatting.

   f. **Point the mouse pointer at the boundary between the column C and column D headings, and then drag to the right until the YTD total fits within its cell.**

3. **Change the format of the numerical values for the YTD region so they appear in USD.**

   a. **Select cell H7, press and hold Shift, and then click cell J10** to select these cells.

   b. **Right-click, and then choose Format Cells** to open the Format Cells dialog box.

   c. From the Category list, **select Currency.**

   d. From the Negative Numbers list, **select the red ($1234.10).**

   e. **Click OK** to apply the formatting.

4. **Change the format of the date so that it appears in the Day-Month-Year format, and then save your work.**

   a. **Right-click cell A2, and then choose Format Cells** to open the Format Cells dialog box.

   b. From the Type list, **select 14-Mar-01, and then click OK** to apply the formatting.

   Type:

   ```
   *3/14/2001
   *Wednesday, March 14, 2001
   3/14
   3/14/01
   03/14/01
   14-Mar
   14-Mar-01
   ```

   Locale (location):

   c. **Click the Save button.**

TOPIC F

Create a Custom Number Format

You have applied number formats to cell contents. But now you realize that Excel's standard number formats do not meet your business needs for some of your worksheets. In this topic, you will create a custom number format.

Imagine you work for a company that uses nine digits for its Employee ID number. The numbers take the following format: ###-##-##-##. Excel doesn't provide the exact number format that you want for that data. By creating a custom number format, you make it easier to enter numeric data that's specific to your unique application.

How to Create a Custom Number Format

Procedure Reference: Create a Custom Number Format

To create a custom number format:

1. Choose Format→Cells to open the Format Cells dialog box.

2. On the Number tab, from the Category list, select Custom.

3. Either type a new custom format from scratch in the Type text box, or select one of the existing models from the list and modify it as needed.

4. Click OK to apply the format.

ACTIVITY 4-6

Creating a Custom Number Format

Objective:
To create a custom number format.

Setup:
Activity 4-5 is complete. The file Calculations is open.

Scenario:
You have a range of data that includes Employee IDs. You want to format the data, but none of the existing number format categories that Excel provides is appropriate. You decide to create your own custom number format. Here is an example of what you want the Employee IDs to look like: *SS123-456-789.*

What You Do	How You Do It
1. **Create the custom number format.**	a. **Select cell B7, and then choose Format→Cells** to open the Format Cells dialog box.
	b. On the Number tab, from the Category list, **select Custom.**
	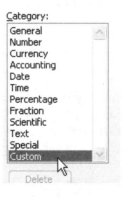
	c. **Double-click in the Type text box to select its contents, and then type** *"SS"###-###-###*
	Type: "SS"###-###-###

d. **Click OK** to apply the formatting.

```
SS123-456-789
```

2. **Copy the custom number format to the remaining Employee IDs, and then save your work.**

a. **Drag the fill handle from cell B7 to cell B10** to fill the remaining cells with the same value.

b. **Click the drop-down arrow next to the Auto Fill Options button.**

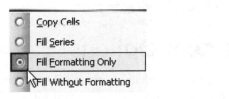

c. **Select Fill Formatting Only** to copy only the formatting from the originating cell to the destination cells.

d. **Click the Save button.**

TOPIC G

Align Cell Contents

One of the ways you have formatted cell contents is by changing font size and type. Another formatting decision you might have to make is where the contents of a cell appear within the cell. In this topic, you will align cell contents.

The following figure, Figure 4-18, shows a heading for a column of data that doesn't line up with the data underneath. Aligning cell contents gives your worksheets a neat and professional look that makes the data easier to read, as shown in Figure 4-19.

April
$135.15
$205.79
$310.44
$250.15

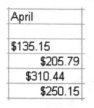

Figure 4-18: *Cell contents that are not aligned.*

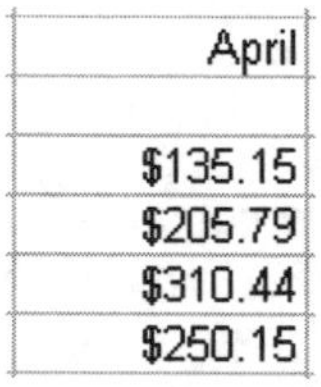
April
$135.15
$205.79
$310.44
$250.15

Figure 4-19: *Cell contents that are aligned.*

Alignment Options

You can align cell contents horizontally or vertically in a variety of ways. The following figure, Figure 4-20, shows the Alignment tab of the Format Cells dialog box.

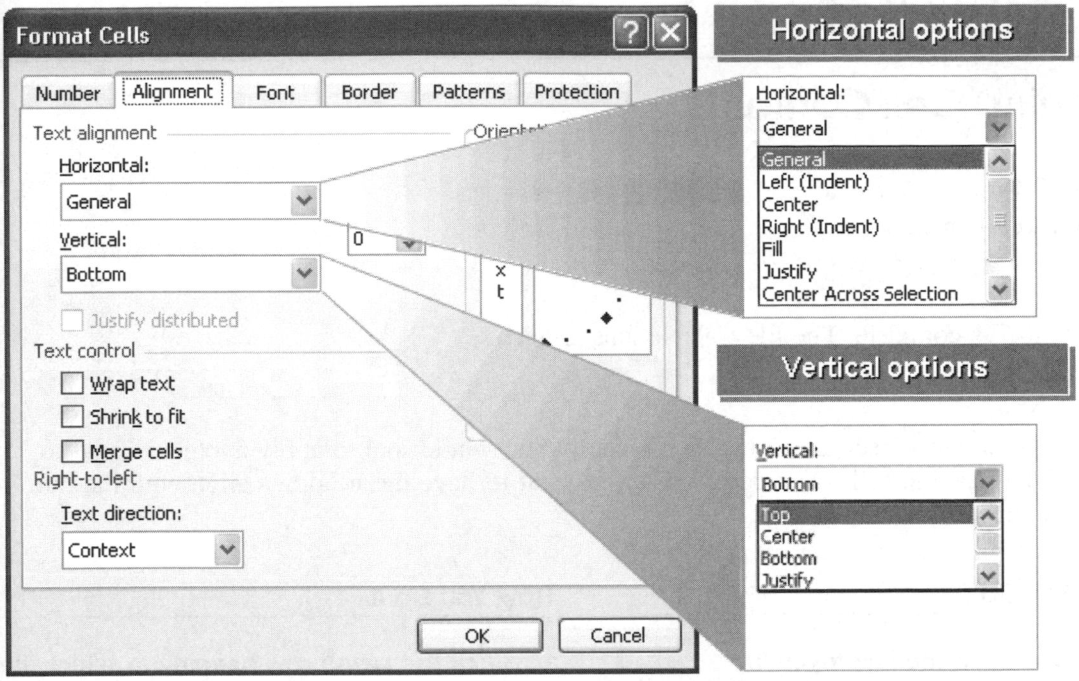

Figure 4-20: *The Alignment tab of the Format Cells dialog box.*

How to Align Cell Contents

Procedure Reference: Align Cell Contents

To align cell contents:

1. Select the cell(s) whose contents you want to align.

2. Either click one of the Align buttons on the formatting toolbar, or choose Format→Cells to open the Format Cells dialog box.

3. Click the Alignment tab.

4. Under Text Alignment, select your desired alignment.

5. Click OK to apply the alignment.

ACTIVITY 4-7

Aligning Cell Contents

Objective:
To align cell contents.

Setup:
Activity 4-6 is complete. The file Calculations is open.

Scenario:
The sales data worksheet is coming along nicely. You would like to apply another format to some of the heading cells. You decide that you want to have the headings align with the numbers that appear below them.

What You Do	How You Do It
1. **Right-align the Employee ID, Months, and YTD headings.**	a. **Click the row 5 row heading** to select the entire row.
	b. On the Formatting toolbar, **click the Align Right button** [icon] to right-align the contents of the row.
2. **Right-align the Monthly Totals, Monthly Average, Highest, and Lowest headings, and then save your work.**	a. **Select cell B12, press and hold Shift, and then click cell B16** to select these cells.
	b. **Choose Format→Cells** to open the Format Cells dialog box.
	c. **Click the Alignment tab** to view the cell alignment options.
	d. In the Text Alignment region, from the Horizontal drop-down list, **select Right (Indent).**

Text alignment

Horizontal:

General ∨
General
Left (Indent)
Center
Right (Indent)
Fill
Justify
Center Across Selection

e. **Click OK** to apply the alignment.

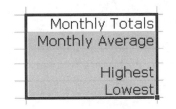

f. **Click in any empty cell** to deselect the selected cells.

g. **Click the Save button.**

TOPIC H

Find and Replace Formats

You have found and replaced cell data. Now you need to change the formatting of a subset of cells inside a worksheet. In this topic, you will find and replace formats.

Suppose you have a worksheet that contains the same formatting on a variety of cells. You realize that the format you've applied to some of the cells is incorrect. By finding and replacing formats in the same way you find and replace cell data, you can be assured that you won't miss any instances, as you might if you tried to make the changes manually.

How to Find and Replace Formats

Procedure Reference: Find and Replace Formats

To find and replace formats:

1. Choose Edit→Replace to open the Find And Replace dialog box.

2. Click Options to expand the Find And Replace options.

3. On the Find What line, click the Format button to open the Find Format dialog box.

4. In the Find Format dialog box, locate and select the format you want to find in the workbook.

5. Click OK to return to the Find And Replace dialog box.

6. On the Replace With line, click the Format button to open the Replace Format dialog box.

7. In the Replace Format dialog box, locate and select or create the new format you want to apply to the workbook.

8. Click OK to return to the Find And Replace dialog box.

9. In the Find And Replace dialog box, click Find Next to locate the first instance of the existing format.

10. In the Find And Replace dialog box, click Replace (or Replace All) to replace the old format with the new format.

11. Click OK to confirm the replacements.

12. Close the Find And Replace dialog box.

ACTIVITY 4-8

Finding and Replacing Formats

Objective:

To find and replace formats.

Setup:

Activity 4-7 is complete. The file Calculations is open. Any empty cell is selected.

Scenario:

You are still working on the sales data worksheet. Your manager has decided to change the format of the Employee ID numbers from *SS###-###-###* to *EID-##-###-###-#*. This new number matches the standard employee number format for all employees in your company.

What You Do	How You Do It
1. Locate the existing format.	a. Choose Edit→**Replace** to open the Find And Replace dialog box.
	b. **Drag to select the contents of the Find What text box, and then press Delete.**
	c. **Drag to select the contents of the Replace With text box, and then press Delete.**

d. **Click Options** to display more options in the dialog box.

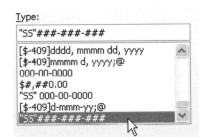

e. On the Find What line, **click Format** to open the Find Format dialog box.

f. **Click the Number tab, and then, from the Category list, select Custom.**

g. **Scroll to the bottom of the Type list, and select "SS"###-###-###.**

Type:

```
"SS"###-###-###

[$-409]dddd, mmmm dd, yyyy
[$-409]mmmm d, yyyy;@
000-00-0000
$#,##0.00
"SS" 000-00-0000
[$-409]d-mmm-yy;@
"SS"###-###-###
```

h. **Click OK.**

---

2. **Create the new custom format.**

a. In the Find And Replace dialog box, on the Replace With line, **click Format** to open the Replace Format dialog box with the Number tab already selected.

b. From the Category list, **select Custom.**

LESSON 4

c. **Double-click in the Type text box** to select its contents, and then **type** *"EID"-##-###-###-#*

Type:

```
"EID"-##-###-###-#
```

d. **Click OK.**

3. **Replace the existing format with the new format, and then save your work.**

a. In the Find And Replace dialog box, **click Find Next** to locate and select the first instance of the old format.

Employee ID
SS123-456-789

b. In the Find And Replace dialog box, **click Replace** to replace the first instance of the old format with the new format.

Employee ID
EID-12-345-678-9
SS234-567-890

c. In the Find And Replace dialog box, **click Replace All** to replace the remaining instances of the old format with the new format and open a dialog box confirming the replacements.

Employee ID
EID-12-345-678-9
EID-23-456-789-0
EID-34-567-890-1
EID-45-678-901-2

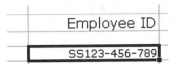

Microsoft Excel

Excel has completed its search and has made 3 replacements.

OK

d. In the dialog box that confirms the replacements, **click OK.**

e. In the Find And Replace dialog box, **click Close.**

f. **Click the Save button.**

TOPIC I

Apply an AutoFormat

You have made a variety of formatting changes to a worksheet. Now you would like to speed up the process of formatting worksheets. In this topic, you will apply an AutoFormat.

Imagine you have a worksheet that you need to format quickly. Due to time constraints, you don't have the time to format the worksheet by hand. AutoFormat allows you to quickly change the format of selected cells or an entire worksheet.

AutoFormat

Definition:

AutoFormats are a predefined group of formats that you can apply to a range of data. AutoFormats include such formatting options as font size, patterns, and alignment.

Example: AutoFormats

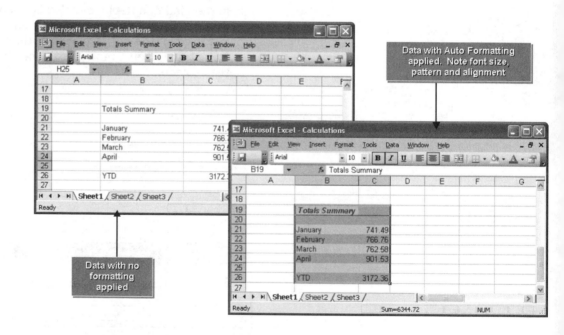

How to Apply an AutoFormat

Procedure Reference: Apply an AutoFormat

To apply an AutoFormat:

1. Select the range of cells to which you want to apply the AutoFormat.

2. Choose Format→AutoFormat to open the AutoFormat dialog box.

3. Select the AutoFormat you want to apply.

4. Click OK to apply the AutoFormat.

ACTIVITY 4-9

Applying an AutoFormat

Objective:
To apply an AutoFormat.

Setup:
Activity 4-8 is complete. The file Calculations is open.

Scenario:
You are about to wrap up development on the sales data worksheet. Your manager has just come into your office and let you know that she has received a request to format this worksheet in the same way as other worksheets in other groups. She hands you a copy of another worksheet and you realize that the format of this new worksheet is one of the stock AutoFormats available within Excel. You decide to apply this AutoFormat (which you have identified as AutoFormat List 1) to your sales data worksheet.

What You Do	How You Do It
1. Apply an AutoFormat to the cells in the worksheet.	a. Select cell A1, press and hold Shift, and then click cell J26 to select this range of cells.
	b. Choose Format→AutoFormat to open the AutoFormat dialog box.

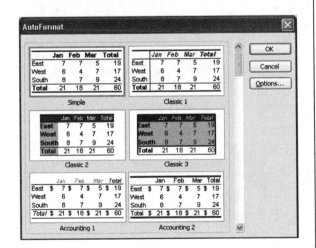

LESSON 4

c. **Scroll to and then select the List 1 AutoFormat.**

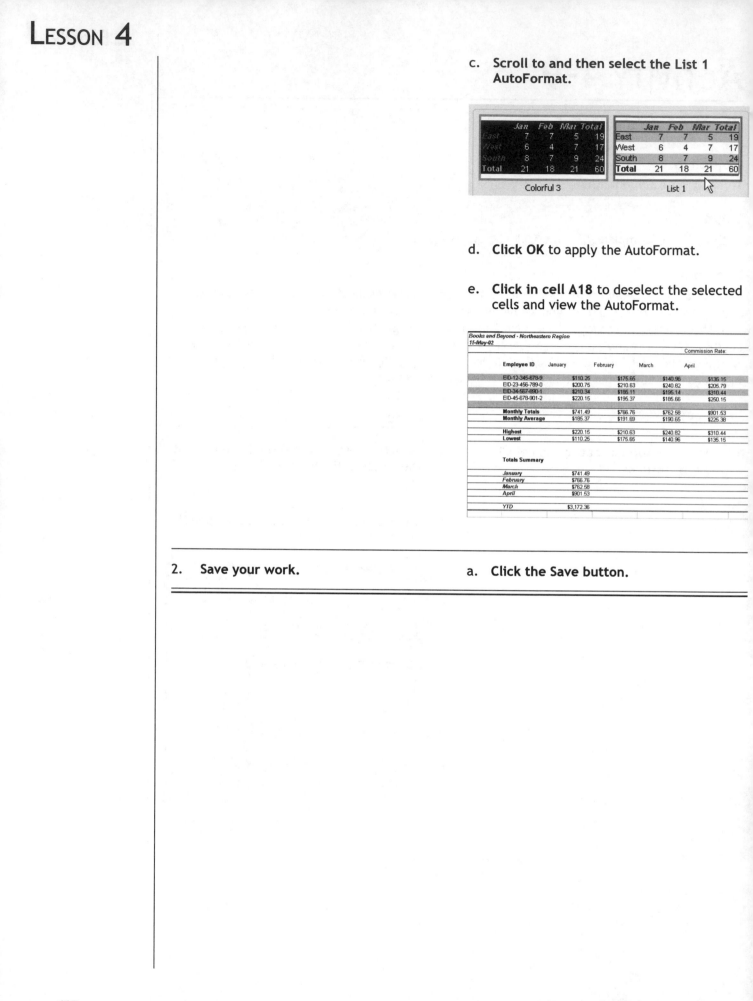

d. **Click OK** to apply the AutoFormat.

e. **Click in cell A18** to deselect the selected cells and view the AutoFormat.

2. **Save your work.**

a. **Click the Save button.**

TOPIC J

Apply Styles

You have applied an AutoFormat to quickly format a spreadsheet. Now you would like to apply specific formats to various cells. In this topic, you will apply styles.

You have many cells whose contents you would like to align in the middle of the cell. You can save considerable amounts of development time if you apply a style to these cells—rather than format the cells individually. Additionally, if you apply a style to the cells and later decide to change the format in the style, you would just have to change the style in one place and every cell would change to the new format.

Styles

Definition:

A *style* is a collection of individual format options that you can apply at the same time to selected cells. You can use a predefined style or create and name custom styles of your own. Each style can include the following elements:

- Number
- Alignment
- Font
- Border
- Patterns
- Protection

Example:

The following figures, Figure 4-21 and Figure 4-22, show some examples of a worksheet before and after a style has been applied.

	A	B	C	D	E	F	G	H	I
1				CIRCA Company Employee Information					
2									
3									
4	NUM	FIRST	LAST	EMP#	DIVISION	DEPT	DATE of HIRE	BEN	HRS
5	1	Sara	Kling	GW29	Maine	Sales	24-Dec-1986	R	35.5
6	2	Sean	Willis	GBW09	Connecticut	Sales	5-Jul-1985	D	35.5
7	3	Colleen	Abel	CW58	New Hampsh	Sales	26-Jul-1990	DRH	42
8	4	Teri	Binga	AW55	Vermont	Sales	7-Jun-1988	RH	40
9	5	Frank	Culbert	GBC07	Connecticut	Development	12-Jun-1983	DRH	40
10	6	Kristen	DeVinney	GBS45	Connecticut	Staff	5-Jun-1987	D	35
11	7	Theresa	Califano	CW19	New Hampsh	Sales	26-Feb-1989	RH	35
12	8	Barry	Bally	GC04	Maine	Development	15-Apr-1983	D	40

Figure 4-21: *A range of cells with no style.*

	A	B	C	D	E	F	G	H	I
1				CIRCA Company Employee Information					
2									
3									
4	NUM	FIRST	LAST	EMP#	DIVISION	DEPT	DATE of HIRE	BEN	HRS
5	1	Sara	Kling	GW29	Maine	Sales	24-Dec-1986	R	35.5
6	2	Sean	Willis	GBW09	Connecticut	Sales	5-Jul-1985	D	35.5
7	3	Colleen	Abel	CW58	ew Hampshire	Sales	26-Jul-1990	DRH	42
8	4	Teri	Binga	AW55	Vermont	Sales	7-Jun-1988	RH	40
9	5	Frank	Culbert	GBC07	Connecticut	Development	12-Jun-1983	DRH	40
10	6	Kristen	DeVinney	GBS45	Connecticut	Staff	5-Jun-1987	D	35
11	7	Theresa	Califano	CW19	ew Hampshire	Sales	26-Feb-1989	RH	35
12	8	Barry	Bally	GC04	Maine	Development	15-Apr-1983	D	40
13	9	Cheryl	Halal	CA26	ew Hampshire	Research	1-Feb-1990	DR	35.5

Figure 4-22: *A range of cells with a style applied.*

How to Apply Styles

Procedure Reference: Apply a Style

To apply a style:

1. Select the range of cells to which you would like to apply the style.

2. Choose Format→Style to open the Style dialog box.

3. In the Style dialog box, either accept the default style (Normal) or select a new style.

4. In the Style dialog box, click OK to apply the style.

Procedure Reference: Modify a Style

To modify a style:

1. Choose Format→Style to open the Style dialog box.

2. In the Style dialog box, either accept the default style (Normal) or select the style you want to modify.

3. Click Modify to open the Format Cells dialog box.

4. In the Format Cells dialog box, make modifications as needed and then click OK.

5. In the Style dialog box, click OK to apply the style.

ACTIVITY 4-10

Applying a Style

Objective:

To apply a style.

Setup:

Activity 4-9 is complete. The file Calculations is open.

Scenario:

You've formatted the sales data worksheet using an AutoFormat. Now your manager has come to you and said the company no longer wants to use this new format. She needs you to return the worksheet to a non-formatted state so that she can take the raw data to a meeting where the final formatting decisions will be made. You could go cell by cell and remove the formats from each cell, but you remember a faster way to change the formatting of an entire worksheet: you can apply a style that returns the contents of the worksheet to an unformatted state. The only change your manager would like to see is to have the data display in 11 point Verdana italics font.

What You Do	How You Do It
1. Select the data in the worksheet, and then open the Style dialog box.	a. Select cell **A1**, press and hold **Shift**, and then click cell **J26** to select this range of cells.
	b. Choose **Format→Style** to open the Style dialog box with the Normal style selected by default.

2. **Modify the font, and then apply the style.**

   a. In the Style dialog box, **click Modify** to open the Format Cells dialog box.

   b. **Click the Font tab.**

   c. From the Font list box, **select Verdana.**

   d. From the Font Style list box, **select Italic.**

   e. From the Size list box, **select 11.**

Font:	Font style:	Size:
Verdana	Italic	11
Univers Condensed	Regular	8
Verdana	Italic	9
Viner Hand ITC	Bold	10
Vivaldi	Bold Italic	11

   f. In the Format Cells dialog box, **click OK** to return to the Style dialog box.

   g. In the Style dialog box, **click OK** to apply the style.

3. **Save and close your work.**

   a. **Click the Save button.**

   b. **Choose File→Close.**

Lesson 4 Follow-up

In this lesson, you formatted worksheets. Formatting worksheets can visually differentiate one set of data from other sets, making it easier to quickly locate information.

1. **Consider the following worksheet, shown in Figure 4-C. What type of formatting would you apply to this worksheet to make the content easier to read?**

	A	B	C	D	E	F	G	H	I
1	Books and Beyond - Northeastern Region								
2	5/15/2002								
3						Commission Rate:		17%	
4									
5		Employee ID	January	February	March	April		YTD Total	YTD Average
6									
7		123456789	110.25	175.65	140.96	135.15		562.01	140.5025
8		234567890	200.75	210.63	240.82	205.79		857.99	214.4975
9		345678901	210.34	185.11	195.14	310.44		901.03	225.2575
10		456789012	220.15	195.37	185.66	250.15		851.33	212.8325
11									
12		Monthly Totals	741.49	766.76	762.58	901.53			
13		Monthly Average	185.3725	191.69	190.645	225.3825			
14									
15		Highest	220.15	210.63	240.82	310.44			
16		Lowest	110.25	175.65	140.96	135.15			
17									

Figure 4-C: *An unformatted worksheet.*

2. Consider the following worksheet, shown in Figure 4-D. It has too much formatting and much of the formatting is inconsistent. How would you edit this worksheet to tone down the formatting?

	A	B	C	D	E	F	G	H	I
1	**Books and Beyond – Northeastern Region**								
2	5/15/2002								
3						**Commission**		**17%**	
4									
5		**Employee ID**	January	February	March	April		YTD Total	YTD Average
6									
7		123456789	110.25	175.65	140.96	135.15		562.01	140.503
8		234567890	200.75	210.63	240.82	205.79		857.99	214.498
9		345678901	210.34	185.11	195.14	310.44		901.03	225.258
10		456789012	220.15	195.37	185.66	250.15		851.33	212.833
11									
12		Monthly Totals	741.49	766.76	762.58	901.53			
13		Monthly Average	185.3725	191.69	190.645	225.3825			
14									
15		Highest	220.15	210.63	240.82	310.44			
16		Lowest	110.25	175.65	140.96	135.15			
17									

Figure 4-D: *An overly formatted worksheet.*

NOTES

LESSON 5
Developing a Workbook

Lesson Objectives:

In this lesson, you will develop a workbook.

You will:

* Format worksheet tabs.
* Reposition worksheets in a workbook.
* Insert and delete worksheets.
* Copy and paste worksheets.
* Copy a workbook.

Introduction

You have developed single worksheets. You now have a need to store related data that exists on multiple worksheets in a single Excel file. You can do this by organizing multiple worksheets into a single workbook.

Imagine you have quarterly sales data for the previous fiscal year stored in separate files. You don't have to open multiple files to work with related data. You can store multiple worksheets in a single file making it easier for you to manage data, as shown in Figure 5-1.

	A	B	C	D	E	F	G	H	I	J
1	European Division									
2										
3	Item	QTR 1	QTR 2	QTR 3	QTR 4					
4	Hardware	400	800	900	300					
5	Software	200	500	1200	100					
6	Furniture	300	400	1400	300					
7	Accessories	100	300	500	300					
8										
9	Totals:	$1,000	$2,000	$4,000	$1,000					
10										
11										
12										
13										

Summary \ European Division / N American Division / C American Division / Australian Division

Figure 5-1: *A workbook with multiple worksheets.*

TOPIC A

Format Worksheet Tabs

You are familiar with worksheets and their general appearance in the Excel environment. You would now like to make it easier to visually locate a particular worksheet within a workbook. In this topic, you will format worksheet tabs.

You have a workbook that contains information on different departments in your company, as shown in Figure 5-2.

	A	B	C	D	E	F	G	
1	Books and Beyond™ - Northeastern Region							
2								
3		ID		January	February	March		
4		123456789		175.65	140.96	135.15		
5		234567890		210.63	240.82	205.79		
6		345678901		185.11	195.14	310.44		
7		456789012		195.37	215.97	350.15		
8								
9								
10	Books and Beyond - Midwestern Region							
11								
12		ID		January	February	March		
13		567890123		269.33	291.15	205.17		
14		678901234		110.7	133.5	147		
15		789012345		225	264.75	314.04		
16		890123456		240.7	223.5	123.08		
17								
18								

⊓ ◄ ► ⊔ \ Sheet1 / Sheet2 / Sheet3 /

Figure 5-2: *A workbook with multiple worksheets that have not been formatted.*

You want to visually differentiate each worksheet so that you can quickly identify which worksheet corresponds to which department in your company, as shown in Figure 5-3.

	A	B	C	D	E	F	G	
1	Books and Beyond™ - Northeastern Region							
2								
3		ID		January	February	March		
4		123456789		175.65	140.96	135.15		
5		234567890		210.63	240.82	205.79		
6		345678901		185.11	195.14	310.44		
7		456789012		195.37	215.97	350.15		
8								
9								
10	Books and Beyond - Midwestern Region							
11								
12		ID		January	February	March		
13		567890123		269.33	291.15	205.17		
14		678901234		110.7	133.5	147		
15		789012345		225	264.75	314.04		
16		890123456		240.7	223.5	123.08		
17								
18								

⊓ ◄ ► ⊔ \ Q1 SALES / Q2 SALES / Q3 SALES / Q4 SALES /

Figure 5-3: *A workbook with multiple worksheets that are formatted.*

Changing the name and color of the worksheet tabs allows you to enhance the workbook's readability by further organizing the data into logical chunks.

How to Format Worksheet Tabs

Procedure Reference: Change the Name of a Worksheet Tab

To change the name of a worksheet tab:

1. Select the worksheet you want to change.

2. To enable renaming of the worksheet, do one of the following:

    *   Choose Format→Sheet→Rename.

    *   Right-click the sheet tab and choose Rename.

    *   Double-click the tab.

3. Type the worksheet's new name.

4. Press Enter.

Procedure Reference: Change the Color of a Worksheet Tab

To change the color of a worksheet tab:

1. Select the worksheet you want to change.

2. To enable recoloring of the sheet tab, do one of the following:

    *   Right-click the sheet tab and choose Tab Color.

    *   Choose Format→Sheet→Tab Color to open the Format Tab Color dialog box, and then continue to step 3.

3. Select the desired color.

4. Click OK to apply the color.

ACTIVITY 5-1

Formatting Worksheet Tabs

Objective:

To format worksheet tabs.

Data Files:

*   MultisheetWorkbook

Setup:

No files are open in Excel.

Scenario:

Your manager has just given you the task of keeping the department information (which is stored in an Excel workbook) organized and updated. The workbook (MultisheetWorkbook) consists of four different divisions in your department, as well as a summary page. Your manager would like each worksheet to be color coded and named with a useful name that identifies the contents of the worksheet (something other than Sheet1 or Sheet2, for example).

What You Do	How You Do It
1. In the MultisheetWorkbook file, **rename the first worksheet.**	a. **Choose File→Open** to display the Open dialog box.
	b. **Double-click the MultisheetWorkbook file name.**
	c. **Right-click the Sheet1 tab, and then select Rename** to enable renaming of the tab.

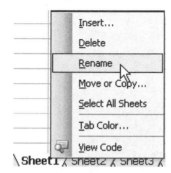

	d. **Type *Australian Division* and press Enter** to rename the tab.

\Australian Division / Sheet2 / Sheet3 / Sheet4 / Sheet5 /

2. **Rename the second worksheet.**	a. **Double-click the Sheet2 tab** to enable renaming of the tab.

\Sheet2 / S

	b. **Type *European Division* and press Enter** to rename the tab.

\European Division / Sheet3 /

3. **Rename the third worksheet.**	a. **Click the Sheet3 tab** to select the worksheet.
	b. **Choose Format→Sheet→Rename** to enable renaming of the tab.

c. **Type *N American Division* and press Enter** to rename the tab.

n ⟍N American Division ⟋ Sheet4 ⟋

---

4. **Rename the fourth and fifth worksheets.**

a. **Double-click the Sheet4 tab** to enable renaming of the tab.

b. **Type *S American Division* and press Enter** to rename the tab.

c. **Double-click the Sheet5 tab** to enable renaming of the tab.

d. **Type *Summary* and press Enter** to rename the tab.

⟍ Australian Division ⟋ European Division ⟋ N American Division ⟋ S American Division ⟍**Summary** ⟋

---

5. **Change the color of the Summary tab.**

a. **Right-click the Summary tab.**

b. **Select Tab Color** to open the Format Tab Color dialog box.

c. **Click Yellow.**

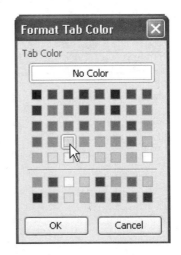

d. **Click OK** to apply the color.

6.	Change the color of the S American Division tab.	a.	Click the S American Division tab to select the worksheet.
		b.	Choose Format→Sheet→Tab Color to open the Format Tab Color dialog box.
		c.	Click Bright Green, and then click OK to apply the color.

7.	Change the colors of the remaining tabs, and then save your work.	a.	Right-click the N American Division tab.
		b.	Select Tab Color, click Light Gray, and then click OK to apply the color.
		c.	Right-click the European Division tab.
		d.	Select Tab Color, click Red, and then click OK to apply the color.
		e.	Right-click the Australian Division tab.
		f.	Select Tab Color, click Purple, and then click OK to apply the color.
		g.	Click the Save button.

TOPIC B

Reposition Worksheets in a Workbook

You have formatted worksheet tabs to better identify the contents of each worksheet. You would now like to rearrange the order of the worksheets in your workbook. In this topic, you will reposition worksheets in a workbook.

Which workbook, the one shown in Figure 5-4 or the one shown in Figure 5-5, has a better order for its worksheets?

Figure 5-4: *A workbook with worksheets that seem out of order.*

Figure 5-5: *A workbook with worksheets that follow a logical order.*

Repositioning worksheets in a workbook allows you to create worksheets as needed and then order them in a logical manner.

How to Reposition Worksheets in a Workbook

Procedure Reference: Reposition Worksheets in a Workbook by Dragging

To reposition worksheets in a workbook:

1. Click and hold the tab of the worksheet you want to move.

2. Drag the worksheet tab to its new position.

3. Release the mouse button.

Procedure Reference: Reposition Worksheets in a Workbook by Using the Move Or Copy Menu Command

To reposition worksheets in a workbook:

1. Select the worksheet you want to move.

2. Choose Edit→Move Or Copy to open the Move Or Copy dialog box.

3. From the To Book list, select the workbook you want to copy the worksheet to.

4. From the Before Sheet list, select the worksheet you want to move immediately to the right of the newly moved worksheet.

5. Click OK.

ACTIVITY 5-2

Repositioning Worksheets in a Workbook

Objective:
To reposition worksheets in a workbook.

Setup:
Activity 5-1 is complete. The file MultisheetWorkbook is open.

Scenario:
You have named and added a color to your sheet tabs to organize them. You now want to further organize the worksheets by rearranging them. Because you use the Summary worksheet the most, you want to move it to the first position. Additionally, the European Division and the N American Division sheets are the most used of the remaining sheets, so you want to position them in the second and third positions, respectively. Finally, the S American Division sheet should appear in the fourth position.

What You Do	How You Do It
1. Move the Summary worksheet to the first position.	a. **Right-click the Summary tab, and then select Move Or Copy** to open the Move Or Copy dialog box with the current workbook selected by default in the To Book drop-down list box, and the Australian Division worksheet selected by default in the Before Sheet list.

b. **Click OK** to move the Summary worksheet to the first position.

2. Move the European Division worksheet to the second position.	a. **Click and hold the European Division tab** until a small arrow appears near the top-left corner of the tab.
	b. **Drag the worksheet to the left until the downward-pointing arrow points to the left of the Australian Division worksheet tab.**
3. Move the N American Division worksheet to the third position.	a. **Click N American Division tab** to select the worksheet.
	b. **Choose Edit→Move Or Copy Sheet** to open the Move Or Copy dialog box.
	c. From the Before Sheet list box in the Move Or Copy dialog box, **select Australian Division.**
	d. **Click OK** to reposition the worksheet before the Australian Division worksheet.

4. **Move the S American Division worksheet to the fourth position, and then save your work.**

a. **Click and hold the S American Division tab until a small arrow appears near the top-left corner of the tab.**

b. **Drag the worksheet to the left until the downward-pointing arrow points to the left of the Australian Division worksheet tab.**

c. **Click the Save button.**

TOPIC C

Insert and Delete Worksheets

You have worked with a fixed number of worksheets. Now, you want to alter the number of worksheets in a workbook. In this topic, you will insert and delete worksheets.

The workbook shown in Figure 5-6 is a workbook that is supposed to have the sales forecasts for the upcoming fiscal year. After inspecting the workbook, you realize that it is missing the fourth quarter (Q4) worksheet. Additionally, you also notice that there is a worksheet named Marketing Projections. After reviewing the Marketing Projections worksheet, you realize that it shouldn't be in this workbook. You can insert a Q4 worksheet to, and remove the Marketing Projections worksheet from, this workbook, as shown in Figure 5-7.

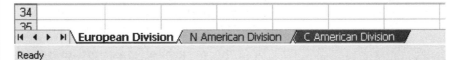

Figure 5-6: *A workbook that needs one worksheet removed and another added.*

Figure 5-7: *The corrected workbook.*

Inserting and deleting worksheets helps you organize by consolidating related data within, and removing extraneous data from, your workbooks.

How to Insert and Delete Worksheets

Procedure Reference: Delete Worksheets

To delete a worksheet from a workbook:

1. Select an existing worksheet.

2. Choose Edit→Delete Sheet to delete the selected worksheet.

Procedure Reference: Inserting Worksheets

To insert a worksheet into a workbook:

1. Select an existing worksheet.

2. Choose Insert→Worksheet to insert the new worksheet to the left of the selected worksheet.

ACTIVITY 5-3

Inserting and Deleting Worksheets

Objective:

To insert and delete worksheets.

Setup:

Activity 5-2 is complete. The file MultisheetWorkbook is open.

Scenario:

The S American Division within your department has recently been moved to a different department. Because you have been given the responsibility of updating the department workbook, you need to delete the S American Division worksheet from the MultisheetWorkbook file. Your manager has also asked you to add a couple of blank worksheets to the MultisheetWorkbook file because she is anticipating some additional divisions being added to your department.

What You Do	How You Do It
1. Delete the S American Division worksheet.	a. With the S American Division worksheet selected, **choose Edit→Delete Sheet** to open a warning dialog box.
	b. **Click Delete** to delete the worksheet.
2. Add two blank worksheets to the workbook, and then save your work.	a. With the Australian Division tab selected, **choose Insert→Worksheet.**

b. **Drag the new Sheet1 tab to the right to position it after the Australian Division tab.**

Australian Division Sheet1

c. **Choose Insert→Worksheet to insert another new worksheet immediately to the left of the Sheet1 worksheet.**

Australian Division Sheet2 Sheet1

d. **Click the Save button.**

TOPIC D

Copy and Paste Worksheets

You have created a worksheet and now need to use it as the starting point for another worksheet. In this topic, you will copy and paste worksheets.

The following figure, Figure 5-8, shows a worksheet you have created that tracks sales for the first quarter of the fiscal year. The worksheet contains all of the formatting and calculations you need.

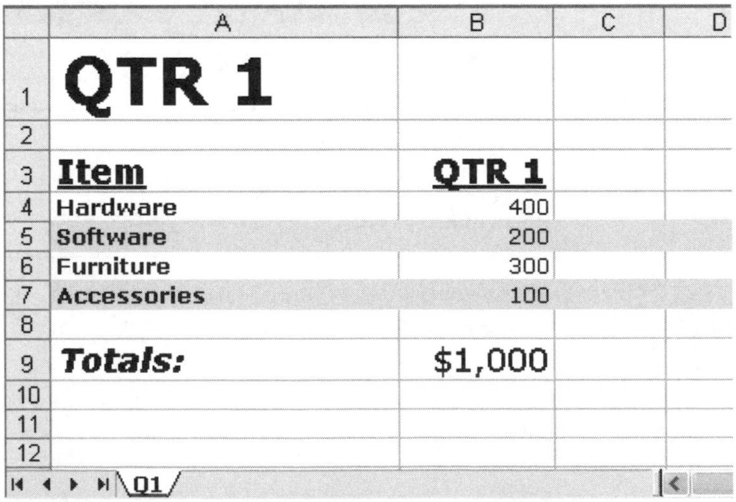

	A	B	C	D
1	**QTR 1**			
2				
3	**Item**	**QTR 1**		
4	Hardware	400		
5	Software	200		
6	Furniture	300		
7	Accessories	100		
8				
9	*Totals:*	**$1,000**		
10				
11				
12				

Q1

Figure 5-8: *A single formatted worksheet.*

Now, you want to create worksheets for the second, third, and fourth quarters, but you want all of these worksheets to have the exact same formatting and calculations, as shown in Figure 5-9.

Figure 5-9: *Multiple worksheets with the same formatting.*

Copying and pasting worksheets eliminates the need to repeat worksheet development for worksheets that share common characteristics.

How to Copy and Paste Worksheets

Procedure Reference: Copy and Paste Worksheets

To copy and paste worksheets:

1. Select the worksheet you want to copy.

2. Choose Edit→Move Or Copy Sheet to open the Move Or Copy dialog box.

3. From the To Book drop-down list, select which workbook you want to copy the worksheet to or accept the default.

4. Check the Create A Copy check box.

5. From the Before Sheet list, select which sheet you want the copied worksheet pasted in front of.

6. Click OK.

ACTIVITY 5-4

Copying and Pasting Worksheets

Objective:
To copy and paste worksheets.

Setup:
Activity 5-3 is complete. The file MultisheetWorkbook is open.

Scenario:
A new division—the Central American division—has been added to your department. Much of the information to be included in the worksheet for this division is the same as the Australian Division worksheet.

What You Do	How You Do It
1. **Copy the Australian Division worksheet.**	a. **Click the Australian Division tab** to select the worksheet.
	b. **Choose Edit→Move Or Copy Sheet** to open the Move Or Copy dialog box with the current workbook selected by default from the To Book list.
	c. **Check the Create A Copy check box.**
	d. In the Before Sheet list box, **select Australian Division.**

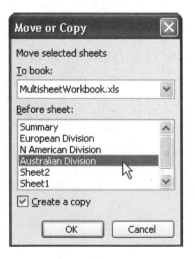

e. **Click OK** to place a copy of the Australian Division worksheet immediately before the existing Australian Division worksheet.

2. **Rename the new worksheet, and change its tab color.**

   a. **Right-click the Australian Division (2) tab.**

   b. **Select Rename.**

   c. **Type** *C American Division* **and press Enter.**

   d. **Right-click the C American Division tab, and then select Tab Color** to open the Format Tab Color dialog box.

   e. **Click Dark Blue.**

   f. **Click OK** to accept the tab color.

3. **Retitle the new worksheet, and then save your work.**

   a. With cell A1 of the C American Division worksheet selected, **drag to select the contents of the Formula Bar.**

   b. **Type** *Central American Division* **and press Enter.**

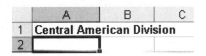

   c. **Click the Save button.**

TOPIC E

Copy a Workbook

You have copied worksheets to create new worksheets. Now you want to reuse the contents of an entire workbook as the basis for a new workbook. In this topic, you will copy a workbook.

You are developing a series of workbooks that will contain the sales forecasts for the next three years. You have just completed building the first workbook and have named it Year 1. Rather than build the Year 2 workbook from scratch, you have decided to copy the Year 1 workbook so that you can quickly convert it into the Year 2 and Year 3 workbooks, respectively. Copying workbooks that share similar formatting can dramatically decrease development time because all of the formatting work is developed once.

How to Copy a Workbook

Procedure Reference: Copy a Workbook from Within Excel

To copy a workbook from within Excel:

1. With the workbook you want to copy open in Excel, hold down Shift or Ctrl and click every worksheet tab in the workbook.

2. Choose Edit→Move Or Copy Sheet to open the Move Or Copy dialog box.

3. Check the Create A Copy check box.

4. From the To Book drop-down list, select (New Book).

5. Click OK.

Procedure Reference: Copy a Workbook from Within Windows Explorer

To copy a workbook from within Windows Explorer:

1. In Windows Explorer, navigate to the directory that contains the workbook file you want to copy.

2. Select the file name.

3. Choose Edit→Copy.

4. In Windows Explorer, navigate to the directory where you want to paste the copy.

5. Choose Edit→Paste.

ACTIVITY 5-5

Copying a Workbook

Objective:

To copy a workbook.

Setup:

Activity 5-4 is complete. The file MultisheetWorkbook is open.

Scenario:

In an effort to maintain uniformity across multiple departments, your department's workbook has been chosen as a template for other departments to use in their workbook development process. Your manager has asked you to make a copy of the MultisheetWorkbook file so she can distribute the copy to other managers.

What You Do	How You Do It
1. Select all of the worksheets.	a. Click the Summary tab to select the worksheet.
	b. Press and hold Shift, and then click the Sheet1 tab to select all of the worksheets.

2. **Copy the selected worksheets to a new workbook.**

    a. **Choose Edit→Move Or Copy Sheet** to open the Move Or Copy dialog box.

    b. **Check the Create A Copy check box.**

    c. From the To Book drop-down list, **select (New Book).**

    d. **Click OK** to copy the selected sheets to a new workbook.

3. **Save and close the new workbook.**

    a. **Choose File→Save** to open the Save As dialog box.

    b. In the File Name text box, **type** *MultisheetWorkbook_COPY*

    c. **Click Save.**

    d. **Choose File→Close.**

Lesson 5 Follow-up

In this lesson, you organized multiple worksheets into a single workbook. By storing multiple worksheets in a single file, you don't have to open multiple files to work with related data.

1. You have 4 separate workbook files: Quarterly_Totals, Quarterly_Projections, Highest_ Sales, and Partners. Each workbook contains a single worksheet that has the same name as its parent workbook. How might you organize these separate workbooks into a single workbook?

2. Consider a project you might develop in Excel. What are some of the worksheets you might develop? What will their names be? How might you organize them into a single workbook?

NOTES

LESSON 6
Printing Workbook Contents

Lesson Objectives:

In this lesson, you will print the contents of a workbook.

You will:

*   Set a print title.
*   Create a header and a footer.
*   Set page margins.
*   Change page orientation.
*   Insert and remove page breaks.
*   Print a range.

Introduction

You have developed worksheets and workbooks. You would now like to share the information stored in these files with other people. One way you can share the contents of your worksheets and workbooks is by printing them.

Imagine that you are presenting the sales data in your Excel workbook at a group meeting. Printing allows you to distribute your workbooks when it's not feasible to distribute them electronically.

TOPIC A

Set a Print Title

When printing, you might want a title at the top of each page. You can do this by setting a print title. In this topic, you will set a print title.

You have printed a copy of a worksheet that has many rows. After printing, you realize that all pages after the first one are somewhat confusing because they don't have the main headings at the top of each column, as shown in Figure 6-1.

This is the top of the first printed page.

CIRCA Company Employee Information

NUM	FIRST	LAST	EMP#	DIVISION	DEPT	DATE of HIRE	BEN	HRS
1	Sara	Kling	GW29	Maine	Sales	24-Dec-1986	R	35.5
2	Sean	Willis	GBW09	Connecticut	Sales	5-Jul-1985	D	35.5
3	Colleen	Abel	CW58	New Hampsh	Sales	26-Jul-1990	DRH	42
4	Teri	Binga	AW55	Vermont	Sales			
5	Frank	Culbert	GBC07	Connecticut	Development			
6	Kristen	DeVinney	GBS45	Connecticut	Staff			
7	Theresa	Califano	CW19	New Hampsh	Sales			
8	Barry	Bally	GC04	Maine	Development	15-Apr-1983	D	40
9	Cheryl	Halal	CA26	New Hampsh	Research	1-Feb-1990	DR	35.5
10	Harry	Swayne	GC25	Maine	Development	30-Dec-1990		40
11	Shing	Chen	GBC05	Connecticut	Development	8-Aug-1984	R	35.5
12	Seth	Rose	CC76	New Hampsh	Development	5-Apr-1990	DRH	32
13	Bob	Ambrose	GW14	Maine	Sales	25-Jan-1985	DH	35.5
14	Chris	Hume	GBS59	Connecticut	Staff	12-May-1988	DH	40
15	Robert	Murray	GRW47	Connecticut	Sales	10-Jun-1987	DH	40

This row contains titles that provide relevance for the columns they are heading.

47	Anne	Davidson	CC23	New Hampsh	Development	6-Apr-1986	RH	25
48	Doug	Briscoll	CA40	New Hampsh	Research	26-May-1987	R	38
49	George	Feldsott	GW37	Maine	Sales	3-Dec-1987	DRH	35.5
50	Steve	Singer	AS29	Vermont	Staff			
51	Carol	Tucker	GBA14	Connecticut	Research			
52	Henry	Paterson	GC20	Maine	Development			
53	Brooks	Hillen	GBA21	Connecticut	Research			
54	Dominick	Mazza	GBC09	Connecticut	Development	10-Oct-1986		40
55	Jennifer	Snyder	CW30	New Hampsh	Sales	7-Jun-1988		25
56	Joshua	Maccaluso	AW69	Vermont	Sales	23-Jan-1991	DRH	40
57	Bill	Wheeler	GBW05	Connecticut	Sales	14-Aug-1981	R	38
58	Todd	Masters	GBS69	Connecticut	Staff	23-Nov-1989	DR	40
59	Karina	Abel	GW30	Maine	Sales	12-Jan-1987	DH	42
60	Edward	Trelly	AC27	Vermont	Development	17-Jun-1986	DR	40
61	Christina	Lillie	GBA24	Connecticut	Research	29-May-1987	RH	25
62	Michael	Lewis	AW58	Vermont	Sales	27-Apr-1989		15.5
63	Jerry	McDonald	GA08	Maine	Research	7-Jul-1982	DR	40

Figure 6-1: *A printed worksheet with no print titles.*

You would like to see the top row of the worksheet at the top of every page of the printed version, as shown in Figure 6-2.

CIRCA Company Employee Information

NUM	FIRST	LAST	EMP#	DIVISION	DEPT	DATE of HIRE	BEN	HRS
1	Sara	Kling	GW29	Maine	Sales	24-Dec-1986	R	35.5
2	Sean	Willis	GBW09	Connecticut	Sales	5-Jul-1985	D	35.5
3	Colleen	Abel	CW58	New Hampsh	Sales	26-Jul-1990	DRH	42
4	Teri	Binga	AW55	Vermont	Sales			
5	Frank	Culbert	GBC07	Connecticut	Development			
6	Kristen	DeVinney	GBS45	Connecticut	Staff			
7	Theresa	Califano	CW19	New Hampsh	Sales			
8	Barry	Bally	GC04	Maine	Development	15-Apr-1983	D	40
9	Cheryl	Halal	CA26	New Hampsh	Research	1-Feb-1990	DR	35.5
10	Harry	Swayne	GC25	Maine	Development	30-Dec-1990		40
11	Shing	Chen	GBC05	Connecticut	Development	8-Aug-1984	R	35.5
12	Seth	Rose	CC76	New Hampsh	Development	5-Apr-1990	DRH	32
13	Bob	Ambrose	GW14	Maine	Sales	25-Jan-1985	DH	35.5
14	Chris	Hume	GBS59	Connecticut	Staff	12-May-1988	DH	40
15	Robert	Murray	GBW47	Connecticut	Sales	10-Jun-1987	DH	40

This is the top of the
second printed page.

NUM	FIRST	LAST	EMP#	DIVISION	DEPT	DATE of HIRE	BEN	HRS
47	Anne	Davidson	CC23	New Hampsh	Development	6-Apr-1986	RH	25
48	Doug	Briscoll	CA40	New Hampsh	Research	26-May-1987	R	38
49	George	Feldsott	GW37	Maine	Sales	3-Dec-1987	DRH	35.5
50	Steve	Singer	AS29	Vermont	Staff			
51	Carol	Tucker	GBA14	Connecticut	Research			
52	Henry	Paterson	GC20	Maine	Development			
53	Brooks	Hillen	GBA21	Connecticut	Research			
54	Dominick	Mazza	GBC09	Connecticut	Development	10-Oct-1986		40
55	Jennifer	Snyder	CW30	New Hampsh	Sales	7-Jun-1988		25
56	Joshua	Maccaluso	AW69	Vermont	Sales	23-Jan-1991	DRH	40
57	Bill	Wheeler	GBW05	Connecticut	Sales	14-Aug-1981	R	38
58	Todd	Masters	GBS69	Connecticut	Staff	23-Nov-1989	DR	40
59	Karina	Abel	GW30	Maine	Sales	12-Jan-1987	DH	42
60	Edward	Trelly	AC27	Vermont	Development	17-Jun-1986	DR	40
61	Christina	Lillie	GBA24	Connecticut	Research	29-May-1987	RH	25
62	Michael	Lewis	AW58	Vermont	Sales	27-Apr-1989		15.5
63	Jerry	McDonald	GA08	Maine	Research	7-Jul-1982	DR	40

The title row appears on this
page because it was
designated as a print title.

Figure 6-2: *A printed worksheet with print titles.*

Setting print titles makes the reading of printed copies of workbooks much easier to understand because important rows or columns are repeated on every page of the printout.

Print Titles

Definition:

A *print title* is a row or column selected to repeat on every printed copy of a worksheet. You can select more than one row or column to repeat, but the rows or columns must be contiguous. Print titles that are rows repeat at the top of the printed page. Print titles that are columns repeat at the left of the printed page.

Example: A Print Title

The following figure, Figure 6-3, shows a long worksheet printed without a print title.

This is the top of the
first printed page.

Benjamin of Brussels
International Chocolate Distributors, Inc.
U.S. Sales 2003

Last Name	First Name	Region	Qtr 1	Qtr 2	Qtr 3	Qtr 4	Total
Arman	Simon	East	$ 14,815.00	$ 13,100.00	$ 11,580.00	$ 17,300.00	$ 56,795.00
Bartholomew	Barbara	North	$ 24,500.00	$ 25,600.00	$ 22,000.00	$ 19,000.00	$ 91,100.00
Childs	Alice	West	$ 20,900.00	$ 22,600.00	$ 20,140.00	$ 24,400.00	$ 88,040.00
Greenburg	Linda	East	$ 15,900.00	$ 22,700.00	$ 17,600.00	$ 20,000.00	$ 76,200.00
Lundquist	Sam	North	$ 25,000.00	$ 34,000.00	$ 21,000.00	$ 35,000.00	$ 115,000.00
McTague	Michael	Northwest	$ 24,110.00	$ 54,812.00	$ 15,200.00	$ 25,600.00	$ 119,722.00
Quayle	Antonio	West	$ 25,600.00	$ 48,752.00	$ 30,300.00	$ 22,600.00	$ 127,252.00
Rivena	Orlando	South	$ 22,600.00	$ 58,445.00	$ 16,800.00	$ 22,700.00	$ 120,545.00
Stark	Oscar	Southwest	$ 22,700.00	$ 48,648.00	$ 36,855.00	$ 35,000.00	$ 143,203.00
Unger	Maria	Southwest	$ 23,300.00	$ 24,600.00	$ 21,380.00	$ 15,937.00	$ 85,217.00
Hanover	Caroline	East	$ 23,800.00	$ 27,700.00	$ 12,600.00	$ 35,000.00	$ 99,100.00
Jaen	Enrique	West	$ 54,826.00	$ 598,224.00	$ 24,100.00	$ 28,000.00	$ 705,150.00
Monder	Alana	Southwest	$ 31,200.00	$ 23,100.00	$ 17,700.00	$ 29,300.00	$ 101,300.00
Innoue	Chika	South	$ 50,224.00	$ 17,300.00	$ 15,200.00	$ 14,600.00	$ 97,324.00
Ryan	Maureen	Midwest	$ 15,500.00	$ 19,000.00	$ 30,300.00	$ 22,600.00	$ 87,400.00
Simmonds	Leon	West	$ 30,900.00	$ 24,400.00	$ 16,800.00	$ 24,513.00	$ 96,613.00
Clark	John	East	$ 14,815.00	$ 13,100.00	$ 11,580.00	$ 17,300.00	$ 56,795.00

This is the top of the second printed page.

No rows repeat at the top of this page because no print title has been set.

Saylor	Rachel	East	$ 22,600.00	$ 58,445.00	$ 16,800.00	$ 22,700.00	$ 120,545.00
Wilson	Tom	West	$ 22,700.00	$ 48,648.00	$ 36,855.00	$ 35,000.00	$ 143,203.00
Hartson	Sue	Southwest	$ 23,300.00	$ 24,600.00	21,380.00	15,937.00	85,217.00
Sandler	Cheryl	South	$ 23,800.00	$ 27,700.00			
Silkey	Marilyn	Midwest	$ 54,826.00	$ 75,894.00			
Neff	Chris	West	$ 31,200.00	$ 23,100.00			
Hyder	Jeff	Southwest	$ 5,623.00	$ 17,300.00			
Schwab	Jan	East	$ 15,500.00	$ 19,000.00	$ 30,300.00	$ 22,600.00	$ 87,400.00
Huntt	Marcia	West	$ 30,900.00	$ 24,400.00	$ 16,800.00	$ 24,513.00	$ 96,613.00
Mosher	Lori	Southwest	$ 25,600.00	$ 48,752.00	$ 30,300.00	$ 22,600.00	$ 127,252.00
Watts	Jeannine	South	$ 22,600.00	$ 58,445.00	$ 16,800.00	$ 22,700.00	$ 120,545.00
Chan	Caryl	Midwest	$ 22,700.00	$ 48,648.00	$ 36,855.00	$ 35,000.00	$ 143,203.00
Turk	Peter	West	$ 23,300.00	$ 24,600.00	$ 21,380.00	$ 15,937.00	$ 85,217.00
Hack	Greg	East	$ 23,800.00	$ 27,700.00	$ 12,600.00	$ 35,000.00	$ 99,100.00
Hartman	Bob	West	$ 54,826.00	$ 88,743.00	$ 24,100.00	$ 28,000.00	$ 195,669.00
French	Frank	Southwest	31,200.00	12,447.00	17,700.00	29,300.00	90,647.00

Figure 6-3: *A long worksheet printed without print titles.*

The following figure, Figure 6-4, shows a worksheet that is printed with a print title.

This is the top of the first printed page.

Benjamin of Brussels
International Chocolate Distributors, Inc.
U.S. Sales 2003

Last Name	First Name	Region	Qtr 1	Qtr 2	Qtr 3	Qtr 4	Total
Arman	Simon	East	$ 14,815.00	$ 13,100.00	$ 11,580.00	$ 17,300.00	$ 56,795.00
Bartholomew	Barbara	North	$ 24,500.00	$ 25,600.00	$ 22,000.00	$ 19,000.00	$ 91,100.00
Childs	Alice	West	$ 20,900.00	$ 22,600.00	$ 20,140.00	$ 24,400.00	$ 88,040.00
Greenburg	Linda	East	$ 15,900.00	$ 22,700.00	$ 17,600.00	$ 20,000.00	$ 76,200.00
Lundquist	Sam	North	$ 25,000.00	$ 34,000.00	$ 21,000.00	$ 35,000.00	$ 115,000.00
McTague	Michael	Northwest	$ 24,110.00	$ 54,812.00	$ 15,200.00	$ 25,600.00	$ 119,722.00
Quayle	Antonio	West	$ 25,600.00	$ 48,752.00	$ 30,300.00	$ 22,600.00	$ 127,252.00
Rivena	Orlando	South	$ 22,600.00	$ 58,445.00	$ 16,800.00	$ 22,700.00	$ 120,545.00
Stark	Oscar	Southwest	$ 22,700.00	$ 48,648.00	$ 36,855.00	$ 35,000.00	$ 143,203.00
Unger	Maria	Southwest	$ 23,300.00	$ 24,600.00	$ 21,380.00	$ 15,937.00	$ 85,217.00
Hanover	Caroline	East	$ 23,800.00	$ 27,700.00	$ 12,600.00	$ 35,000.00	$ 99,100.00
Jaen	Enrique	West	$ 54,826.00	$ 598,224.00	$ 24,100.00	$ 28,000.00	$ 705,150.00
Monder	Alana	Southwest	$ 31,200.00	$ 23,100.00	$ 17,700.00	$ 29,300.00	$ 101,300.00
Innoue	Chika	South	$ 50,224.00	$ 17,300.00	$ 15,200.00	$ 14,600.00	$ 97,324.00
Ryan	Maureen	Midwest	$ 15,500.00	$ 19,000.00	$ 30,300.00	$ 22,600.00	$ 87,400.00
Simmonds	Leon	West	$ 30,900.00	$ 24,400.00	$ 16,800.00	$ 24,513.00	$ 96,613.00
Clark	John	East	$ 14,815.00	$ 13,100.00	$ 11,580.00	$ 17,300.00	$ 56,795.00

This is the top of the second printed page.

These rows have been set as a print title and will repeat at the top of every printed page.

Benjamin of Brussels
International Chocolate Distributors, Inc.
U.S. Sales 2003

Last Name	First Name	Region	Qtr 1	Qtr 2	Qtr 3	Qtr 4	Total
Saylor	Rachel	East	$ 22,600.00	$ 58,445.00	$ 16,800.00	$ 22,700.00	$ 120,545.00
Wilson	Tom	West	$ 22,700.00	$ 48,648.00	$ 36,855.00	$ 35,000.00	$ 143,203.00
Hartson	Sue	Southwest	$ 23,300.00	$ 24,600.00	$ 21,380.00	$ 15,937.00	$ 85,217.00
Sandler	Cheryl	South	$ 23,800.00	$ 27,700.00	$ 12,600.00	$ 35,000.00	$ 99,100.00
Silkey	Marilyn	Midwest	$ 54,826.00	$ 75,894.00	$ 24,100.00	$ 28,000.00	$ 182,820.00
Neff	Chris	West	$ 31,200.00	$ 23,100.00	$ 17,700.00	$ 29,300.00	$ 101,300.00
Hyder	Jeff	Southwest	$ 5,623.00	$ 17,300.00	$ 15,200.00	$ 14,600.00	$ 52,723.00
Schwab	Jan	East	$ 15,500.00	$ 19,000.00	$ 30,300.00	$ 22,600.00	$ 87,400.00
Huntt	Marcia	West	$ 30,900.00	$ 24,400.00	$ 16,800.00	$ 24,513.00	$ 96,613.00
Mosher	Lori	Southwest	$ 25,600.00	$ 48,752.00	$ 30,300.00	$ 22,600.00	$ 127,252.00
Watts	Jeannine	South	$ 22,600.00	$ 58,445.00	$ 16,800.00	$ 22,700.00	$ 120,545.00
Chan	Caryl	Midwest	$ 22,700.00	$ 48,648.00	$ 36,855.00	$ 35,000.00	$ 143,203.00

Figure 6-4: *A long worksheet with print titles that repeat on each page of the printed document.*

How to Set a Print Title

Procedure Reference: Set a Print Title

To set a print title:

1. Choose File→Page Setup to open the Page Setup dialog box.

2. Click the Sheet tab to view the available options.

3. In the Print Titles region of the Page Setup dialog box, click the selection button to the right of the Rows To Repeat At Top text box.

4. On the worksheet, draw a selection marquee around the range of cells you want as a print title or accept the default.

5. Press Enter to accept this range as your Print Title.

6. In the Page Setup dialog box, click OK to accept the changes.

ACTIVITY 6-1

Setting a Print Title

Objective:
To set a print title.

Data Files:
• PrintPractice

Setup:
Close any open files. Open the file PrintPractice.

Scenario:
Your worksheet contains too many rows to print neatly on a single page. You want to print all the rows so that your column headings repeat on every page.

What You Do	How You Do It
1. Set the print title.	a. **Choose File→Page Setup** to open the Page Setup dialog box.
	b. **Click the Sheet tab** to view the available options.
	c. In the Print Titles region of the Page Setup dialog box, **click the selection button ▦ to the right of the Rows To Repeat At Top text box** to automatically minimize the Page Setup dialog box and draw a selection marquee around the contents of row 4 because this row was selected by default.
	d. **Press Enter** to accept this range as your Print Title.
	e. **Click OK** to accept the changes.
2. Preview the print version of the worksheet.	a. **Choose File→Print Preview** to open the PrintPractice file in a preview window.
	b. On the vertical scroll bar, **click the downward-pointing scroll arrow** to view the second page of the printout.

Last Name	First Name	Region	Qtr 1	Qtr 2	Qtr 3
Decker	Janet	Southwest	$ 15,900.00	$ 22,700.00	$ 17,600.00
Hurley	Arica	South	$ 25,000.00	$ 34,000.00	$ 21,000.00
Chaffee	Angela	Midwest	$ 24,110.00	$ 54,812.00	$ 15,200.00
Schimkee	Adam	West	$ 25,600.00	$ 48,752.00	$ 30,300.00
Greenburg	Gail	Southwest	$ 22,600.00	$ 58,445.00	$ 16,800.00
Womble	Anna	South	$ 22,700.00	$ 48,648.00	$ 36,855.00

	c. In the preview window, **click Close**.

3. **Print the workbook.**

    a. **Choose File→Print** to open the Print dialog box.

    b. Under Print What, **select Entire Workbook.** For the purposes of this course, you will not actually send this file to the printer. If you were going to print it, you would click OK at this point.

    c. **Click Cancel.**

Topic B

Create a Header and a Footer

When printing a worksheet, you might want page numbers or other information to appear at the top or bottom of each page. In this topic, you will create a header and a footer.

Which printout, the one shown in Figure 6-5 or the one shown in Figure 6-6, makes it easy to identify the data being presented?

NUM	FIRST	LAST	EMP#	DIVISION	DEPT	DATE of HIRE	BEN	HRS
1	Sara	Kling	GW29	Maine	Sales	24-Dec-1986	R	35.5
2	Sean	Willis	GBW09	Connecticut	Sales	5-Jul-1985	D	35.5
3	Colleen	Abel	CW58	New Hampsh	Sales	26-Jul-1990	DRH	42
4	Teri	Binga	AW55	Vermont	Sales	7-Jun-1988	RH	40
5	Frank	Culbert	GBC07	Connecticut	Developm	12-Jun-1983	DRH	40
6	Kristen	DeVinney	GBS45	Connecticut	Staff	5-Jun-1987	D	35
7	Theresa	Califano	CW19	New Hampsh	Sales	26-Feb-1989	RH	35
8	Barry	Bally	GC04	Maine	Developm	15-Apr-1983	D	40
9	Cheryl	Halal	CA26	New Hampsh	Research	1-Feb-1990	DR	35.5
10	Harry	Swayne	GC25	Maine	Developm	30-Dec-1990		40
11	Shing	Chen	GBC05	Connecticut	Developm	8-Aug-1984	R	35.5
12	Seth	Rose	CC76	New Hampsh	Developm	5-Apr-1990	DRH	32
13	Bob	Ambrose	GW14	Maine	Sales	25-Jan-1985	DH	35.5
14	Chris	Hume	GBS59	Connecticut	Staff	12-May-1988	DH	40
15	Robert	Murray	GBW47	Connecticut	Sales	10-Jun-1987	DH	40
16	James	Rich	GBC11	Connecticut	Developm	11-Oct-1986	DH	35.5
17	George	Gorski	CA18	New Hampsh	Research	7-May-1985	H	40
18	Paul	Hoffman	GBS57	Connecticut	Staff	19-Dec-1987	H	40
19	Dean	Kramer	AC49	Vermont	Developm	23-Jun-1987	RH	40
20	Carol	Hill	GW18	Maine	Sales	21-Jul-1986		35.5
21	Julia	Smith	GBA19	Connecticut	Research	17-Feb-1984	RH	25
22	Jacqueline	Banks	AS03	Vermont	Staff	2-Feb-1984	H	40
23	Jeffrey	Strong	GW04	Maine	Sales	8-Mar-1981	R	40
24	Jeri Lynn	MacFall	AW07	Vermont	Sales	8-Apr-1984		40
25	Sung	Kim	GA49	Maine	Research	15-Nov-1989	DRH	40
26	Theodore	Ness	CA80	New Hampsh	Research	4-Aug-1991	DRH	32
27	Brad	Hinkelman	GW15	Maine	Sales	8-Nov-1985	H	40
28	Robert	Cuffaro	GBC08	Connecticut	Developm	18-Sep-1983	DRH	40
29	Donald	Reese	CS15	New Hampsh	Staff	17-Aug-1984	H	32
30	Joanne	Parker	AW09	Vermont	Sales	23-Aug-1984	H	40
31	Susan	Drake	GRA34	Connecticut	Research	13-Dec-1989	R	25
32	James	Abel	GBC29	Connecticut	Developm	5-Feb-1991		35
33	Laura	Reagan	GBW77	Connecticut	Sales	12-Aug-1990	RH	35
34	Brian	Smith	GS40	Maine	Staff	5-Nov-1988	D	40
35	Mary	Barber	GW32	Maine	Sales	25-Nov-1987	D	35.5
36	Peter	Allen	AW24	Vermont	Sales	31-May-1986		40
37	Mary	Altman	GC12	Maine	Developm	9-Sep-1987	H	29.5
38	Fred	Mallory	CA06	New Hampsh	Research	17-Jun-1983	D	38
39	Molly	Steadman	GBC65	Connecticut	Developm	15-Aug-1989	DH	40
40	Greg	Connors	GBC49	Connecticut	Developm	4 Nov-1987		38
41	Kathy	Mayron	GBA29	Connecticut	Research	19-May-1986	DR	40
42	Bill	Simpson	GS07	Maine	Staff	12-Jan-1982		40
43	Michael	Richardson	GBA28	Connecticut	Research	23-Mar-1986	DH	35
44	Melanie	Bowers	AA35	Vermont	Research	5-Dec-1986	DR	15.5
45	Kyle	EarnhSales	GBS16	Connecticut	Staff	8-Oct-1984	H	40
46	Lance	Davies	GBC64	Connecticut	Developm	30-Dec-1988	DRH	32
47	Anne	Davidson	CC23	New Hampsh	Developm	6-Apr-1986	RH	25
48	Doug	Briscoll	CA40	New Hampsh	Research	26-May-1987	R	38
49	George	Feldsott	GW37	Maine	Sales	3-Dec-1987	DRH	35.5

Figure 6-5: *A printout with no header or footer.*

Lesson 6

Employee Information

Employee Information   4/17/2003   CIRCA Corp.

NUM	FIRST	LAST	EMP#	DIVISION	DEPT	DATE of HIRE	BEN	HRS
1	Sara	Kling	GW29	Maine	Sales	24-Dec-1986	R	35.5
2	Sean	Willis	GBW09	Connecticut	Sales	5-Jul-1985	D	35.5
3	Colleen	Abel	CW58	New Hampsh	Sales	26-Jul-1990	DRH	42
4	Teri	Binga	AW55	Vermont	Sales	7-Jun-1988	RH	40
5	Frank	Culbert	GBC07	Connecticut	Developm	12-Jun-1983	DRH	40
6	Kristen	DeVinney	GBS45	Connecticut	Staff	5-Jun-1987	D	35
7	Theresa	Califano	CW19	New Hampsh	Sales	26-Feb-1989	RH	35
8	Barry	Bally	GC04	Maine	Developm	15-Apr-1983	D	40
9	Cheryl	Halal	CA26	New Hampsh	Research	1-Feb-1990	DR	35.5
10	Harry	Swayne	GC25	Maine	Developm	30-Dec-1990		40
11	Shing	Chen	GBC05	Connecticut	Developm	8-Aug-1984	R	35.5
12	Seth	Rose	CC76	New Hampsh	Developm	5-Apr-1990	DRH	32
13	Bob	Ambrose	GW14	Maine	Sales	25-Jan-1985	DH	35.5
14	Chris	Hume	GBS59	Connecticut	Staff	12-May-1988	DH	40
15	Robert	Murray	GBW47	Connecticut	Sales	10-Jun-1987	DH	40
16	James	Rich	GBC11	Connecticut	Developm	11-Oct-1986	DH	35.5
17	George	Gorski	CA18	New Hampsh	Research	7-May-1985	H	40
18	Paul	Hoffman	GBS57	Connecticut	Staff	19-Dec-1987	H	40
19	Dean	Kramer	AC49	Vermont	Developm	23-Jun-1987	RH	40
20	Carol	Hill	GW18	Maine	Sales	21-Jul-1986		35.5
21	Julia	Smith	GBA19	Connecticut	Research	17-Feb-1984	RH	25
22	Jacqueline	Banks	AS03	Vermont	Staff	2-Feb-1984	H	40
23	Jeffrey	Strong	GW04	Maine	Sales	8-Mar-1981	R	40
24	Jeri Lynn	MacFall	AW07	Vermont	Sales	8-Apr-1984		40
25	Sung	Kim	GA49	Maine	Research	15-Nov-1989	DRH	40
26	Theodore	Ness	CA80	New Hampsh	Research	4-Aug-1991	DRH	32
27	Brad	Hinkelman	GW15	Maine	Sales	8-Nov-1985	H	40
28	Robert	Cuffaro	GBC08	Connecticut	Developm	18-Sep-1983	DRH	40
29	Donald	Reese	CS15	New Hampsh	Staff	17-Aug-1984	H	32
30	Joanne	Parker	AW09	Vermont	Sales	23-Aug-1984	H	40
31	Susan	Drake	GBA34	Connecticut	Research	13-Dec-1989	R	25
32	James	Abel	GBC29	Connecticut	Developm	5-Feb-1991		35
33	Laura	Reagan	GBW77	Connecticut	Sales	12-Aug-1990	RH	35
34	Brian	Smith	GS40	Maine	Staff	5-Nov-1988	D	40
35	Mary	Barber	GW32	Maine	Sales	25-Nov-1987	D	35.5
36	Peter	Allen	AW24	Vermont	Sales	31-May-1986		40
37	Mary	Altman	GC12	Maine	Developm	9-Sep-1987	H	29.5
38	Fred	Mallory	CA06	New Hampsh	Research	17-Jun-1983	D	38
39	Molly	Steadman	GBC65	Connecticut	Developm	15-Aug-1989	DH	40
40	Greg	Connors	GBC49	Connecticut	Developm	4-Nov-1987		38
41	Kathy	Mayron	GBA29	Connecticut	Research	19-May-1986	DR	40
42	Bill	Simpson	GS07	Maine	Staff	12-Jan-1982		40
43	Michael	Richardson	GBA28	Connecticut	Research	23-Mar-1986	DH	35
44	Melanie	Bowers	AA35	Vermont	Research	5-Dec-1986	DR	15.5
45	Kyle	Earnh Sales	GBS16	Connecticut	Staff	8-Oct-1984	H	40
46	Lance	Davies	GBC64	Connecticut	Developm	30-Dec-1988	DRH	32
47	Anne	Davidson	CC23	New Hampsh	Developm	6-Apr-1986	RH	25
48	Doug	Briscoll	CA40	New Hampsh	Research	26-May-1987	R	38
49	George	Feldsott	GW37	Maine	Sales	3-Dec-1987	DRH	35.5

Page 1 of 3

Figure 6-6: *A printout with a header and footer.*

Adding a header and footer to a worksheet helps identify worksheet data and keep the printed form of the worksheet organized.

Headers

Definition:

A *header* is a text or graphic block that repeats at the top of each printed page of your workbook. Headers can contain three sections:

- **The Left Section** aligns its contents with the left edge of the page.
- **The Center Section** centers its contents on the page.
- **The Right Section** aligns its contents with the right edge of the page.

Each section can contain text or graphics that remain the same from page to page or text that changes based on criteria such as a page number or date.

Example:

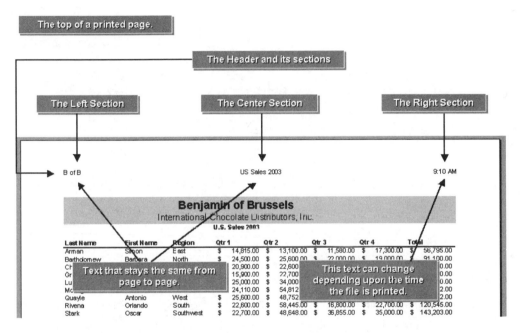

Footers

Definition:

A *footer* is a text or graphic block that repeats at the bottom of each printed page of your workbook. Footers can contain three sections:

- **The Left Section** aligns its contents with the left edge of the page.
- **The Center Section** centers its contents on the page.
- **The Right Section** aligns its contents with the right edge of the page.

Each section can contain text or graphics that remain the same from page to page or text that changes based on criteria such as a page number or date.

Example:

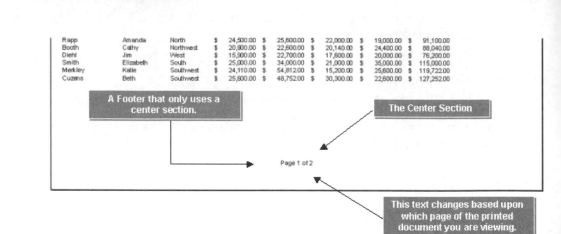

The bottom of a printed page.

A Footer that only uses a center section.

The Center Section

Page 1 of 2

This text changes based upon which page of the printed document you are viewing.

How to Create a Header and a Footer

Procedure Reference: Create a Header

To create a header:

1. Select View→Header And Footer to open the Page Setup dialog box.

2. Select a default header configuration or create a custom header.

    ### To Use a Default Header Configuration

    a. From the Header drop-down list, select a header style.

    ### To Create a Custom Header

    a. Click Custom Header to open the Header dialog box.

    b. Enter the new header data and format it as needed.

    c. Click OK to return to the Page Setup dialog box.

3. Click OK.

Procedure Reference: Create a Footer

To create a footer:

1. Select View→Header And Footer to open the Page Setup dialog box.

2. Select a footer style of your choice or create a custom footer.

    ### To Use a Default Footer Configuration

    a. From the Footer drop-down list, select a footer style.

    ### To Create a Custom Footer

    a. Click Custom Footer to open the Footer dialog box.

    b. Enter the new footer data and format it as needed.

c. Click OK to return to the Page Setup dialog box.

3. Click OK.

ACTIVITY 6-2

Creating a Header and Footer

Objective:

To create a header and a footer.

Setup:

Activity 6-1 is complete. The file PrintPractice is open.

Scenario:

You want to distribute the PrintPractice worksheet during a meeting and you want to make it easy for the meeting participants to keep the printout organized. You decide to provide a header on each page that identifies the printout as the B of B US Sales for 2003. You also decide to add a "Page X of Y" footer to each page.

What You Do	How You Do It
1. Create the header.	a. **Choose View→Header And Footer** to open the Page Setup dialog box.
	b. **Click Custom Header** to open the Header dialog box.

	c. In the Left Section text box, **type *B of B***
	d. In the Center Section text box, **type *US Sales 2003***

e. **Click inside the Right Section text box and then click the Time button** [image].

f. **Click OK.**

---

2. **Create the footer.**

a. In the Page Setup dialog box, from the Footer drop-down list, **select Page 1 Of ?.**

b. **Click OK.**

---

3. **Preview the header and footer.**

a. **Choose File→Print Preview.**

b. **Click Zoom** to increase the magnification and view the header.

c. On the vertical scroll bar, **click the downward-pointing scroll arrow** until you can see the footer.

---

4. **Print the workbook.**

a. **Click Print** to open the Print dialog box. For the purposes of this course, you will not actually send this file to the printer. If you were going to print it, you would click OK at this point.

b. **Click Cancel.**

TOPIC C

Set Page Margins

When printing your worksheet, you want to ensure that the contents of each page do not extend beyond the page margins. In this topic, you will set page margins.

Which printed worksheet is complete, the one shown in Figure 6-7 or the one shown in Figure 6-8?

B of B   US Sales 2003   9:28 AM

Benjamin of Brussels
International Chocolate Distributors, Inc.
U.S. Sales 2003

Last Name	First Name	Region	Qtr 1	Qtr 2	Qtr 3
Arman	Simon	East	$ 14,815.00	$ 13,100.00	$ 11,580.00
Bartholomew	Barbara	North	$ 24,500.00	$ 25,600.00	$ 22,000.00
Childs	Alice	West	$ 20,900.00	$ 22,600.00	$ 20,140.00
Greenburg	Linda	East	$ 15,900.00	$ 22,700.00	$ 17,600.00
Lundquist	Sam	North	$ 25,000.00	$ 34,000.00	$ 21,000.00
McTague	Michael	Northwest	$ 24,110.00	$ 54,812.00	$ 15,200.00
Quayle	Antonio	West	$ 25,600.00	$ 48,752.00	$ 30,300.00
Rivena	Orlando	South	$ 22,600.00	$ 58,445.00	$ 16,800.00
Stark	Oscar	Southwest	$ 22,700.00	$ 48,648.00	$ 36,855.00
Unger	Maria	Southwest	$ 23,300.00	$ 24,600.00	$ 21,380.00
Hanover	Caroline	East	$ 23,800.00	$ 27,700.00	$ 12,600.00
Jaon	Fnrique	West	$ 54,826.00	$ 598,224.00	$ 24,100.00
Monder	Alana	Southwest	$ 31,200.00	$ 23,100.00	$ 17,700.00
Innoue	Chika	South	$ 50,224.00	$ 17,300.00	$ 15,200.00
Ryan	Maureen	Midwest	$ 15,500.00	$ 19,000.00	$ 30,300.00
Simmonds	Leon	West	$ 30,900.00	$ 24,400.00	$ 16,800.00
Clark	John	East	$ 14,815.00	$ 13,100.00	$ 11,580.00
Rapp	Amanda	North	$ 24,500.00	$ 25,600.00	$ 22,000.00
Booth	Cathy	Northwest	$ 20,900.00	$ 22,600.00	$ 20,140.00
Diehl	Jim	West	$ 15,900.00	$ 22,700.00	$ 17,600.00
Smith	Elizabeth	South	$ 25,000.00	$ 34,000.00	$ 21,000.00
Merkley	Katie	Southwest	$ 24,110.00	$ 54,812.00	$ 15,200.00
Cuzens	Beth	Southwest	$ 25,600.00	$ 48,752.00	$ 30,300.00

Figure 6-7: *A printed worksheet that is cut off at the right margin.*

Lesson 6

Benjamin of Brussels
International Chocolate Distributors, Inc.
U.S. Sales 2003

Last Name	First Name	Region	Qtr 1	Qtr 2	Qtr 3	Qtr 4	Total
Arman	Simon	East	$ 14,815.00	$ 13,100.00	$ 11,580.00	$ 17,300.00	$ 56,795.00
Bartholomew	Barbara	North	$ 24,500.00	$ 25,600.00	$ 22,000.00	$ 19,000.00	$ 91,100.00
Childs	Alice	West	$ 20,900.00	$ 22,600.00	$ 20,140.00	$ 24,400.00	$ 88,040.00
Greenburg	Linda	East	$ 15,900.00	$ 22,700.00	$ 17,600.00	$ 20,000.00	$ 76,200.00
Lundquist	Sam	North	$ 25,000.00	$ 34,000.00	$ 21,000.00	$ 35,000.00	$ 115,000.00
McTague	Michael	Northwest	$ 24,110.00	$ 54,812.00	$ 15,200.00	$ 25,600.00	$ 119,722.00
Quayle	Antonio	West	$ 25,600.00	$ 48,752.00	$ 30,300.00	$ 22,600.00	$ 127,252.00
Rivena	Orlando	South	$ 22,600.00	$ 58,445.00	$ 16,800.00	$ 22,700.00	$ 120,545.00
Stark	Oscar	Southwest	$ 22,700.00	$ 48,648.00	$ 36,855.00	$ 35,000.00	$ 143,203.00
Unger	Maria	Southwest	$ 23,300.00	$ 24,600.00	$ 21,380.00	$ 15,937.00	$ 85,217.00
Hanover	Caroline	East	$ 23,800.00	$ 27,700.00	$ 12,600.00	$ 35,000.00	$ 99,100.00
Jaen	Enrique	West	$ 54,826.00	$ 598,224.00	$ 24,100.00	$ 28,000.00	$ 705,150.00
Monder	Alana	Southwest	$ 31,200.00	$ 23,100.00	$ 17,700.00	$ 29,300.00	$ 101,300.00
Innoue	Chika	South	$ 50,224.00	$ 17,300.00	$ 15,200.00	$ 14,600.00	$ 97,324.00
Ryan	Maureen	Midwest	$ 15,500.00	$ 19,000.00	$ 30,300.00	$ 22,600.00	$ 87,400.00
Simmonds	Leon	West	$ 30,900.00	$ 24,400.00	$ 16,800.00	$ 24,513.00	$ 96,613.00
Clark	John	East	$ 14,815.00	$ 13,100.00	$ 11,580.00	$ 17,300.00	$ 56,795.00
Rapp	Amanda	North	$ 24,500.00	$ 25,600.00	$ 22,000.00	$ 19,000.00	$ 91,100.00
Booth	Cathy	Northwest	$ 20,900.00	$ 22,600.00	$ 20,140.00	$ 24,400.00	$ 88,040.00
Diehl	Jim	West	$ 15,900.00	$ 22,700.00	$ 17,600.00	$ 20,000.00	$ 76,200.00
Smith	Elizabeth	South	$ 25,000.00	$ 34,000.00	$ 21,000.00	$ 35,000.00	$ 115,000.00
Merkley	Katie	Southwest	$ 24,110.00	$ 54,812.00	$ 15,200.00	$ 25,600.00	$ 119,722.00
Cuzens	Beth	Southwest	$ 25,600.00	$ 48,752.00	$ 30,300.00	$ 22,600.00	$ 127,252.00

Figure 6-8: *A printed worksheet with useful margins.*

Setting page margins ensures that all of your important data appears on printed copies of your worksheets.

Margin Options

A margin determines the amount of space between the worksheet data and the edge of the paper. There are six adjustable margins. The right and left margins determine the amount of space at the right and left edges of the paper. The top and bottom margins determine the amount of space at the top and bottom of the page. The header and footer margins determine the amount of space between the header or footer and the body of the worksheet printout.

How to Set Page Margins

Procedure Reference: Set Page Margins Using the Page Setup Dialog Box

To set page margins:

1. Choose File→Page Setup to open the Page Setup dialog box.

2. Click the Margins tab.

3. Adjust the margin values as needed.

4. Click OK to apply the margins.

Procedure Reference: Set Page Margins Using the Print Preview Dialog Box

To set page margins:

1. Choose File→Print Preview to open the Print Preview dialog box.

2. Click the Margins button to display the margin guides.

3. Drag the margin guides as needed.

4. Close the Print Preview dialog box.

ACTIVITY 6-3

Setting Page Margins

Objective:
To set page margins.

Setup:
Activity 6-2 is complete. The file PrintPractice is open.

Scenario:
You want to distribute the PrintPractice workbook during a meeting, and you've decided to increase the amount of whitespace on the printed worksheet so that people can make notes right on the page. You decide to provide a larger margin at the bottom of the page for notes. You realize that increasing the bottom whitespace takes away from the amount of space available for data to print on each individual page. You decide to decrease the right and left margins to make up for the increased margin at the bottom of the page.

What You Do	How You Do It
1. Set the bottom margin.	a. Choose File→Page Setup.
	b. Click the Margins tab to view the available options.
	c. In the Bottom scroll box, click the upwards-pointing arrow twice to scroll to the 1.5″ setting.
	Bottom: 1.5
	d. Click OK.
	e. To preview the new setting, click the Print Preview button [ ] .
2. Set the right and left margins.	a. In the print preview window, click Margins to display the margin guides.

b. **Drag the left margin guide to the left** until the margin indicator states Left Margin: 0.25.

c. **Drag the right margin guide to the right** until the margin indicator states Right Margin: 0.25.

3. **Print the active worksheet.**

a. **Click Print** to open the Print dialog box with the Active Sheet(s) option selected by default. For the purposes of this course, you will not actually send this file to the printer. If you were going to print it, you would click OK at this point.

b. **Click Cancel.**

TOPIC D

Change Page Orientation

When printing your worksheet, you might want to change the orientation of the information on the page. In this topic, you will change the page orientation.

Which printout do you prefer, the one shown in Figure 6-9 or the one shown in Figure 6-10?

Benjamin of Brussels
International Chocolate Distributors, Inc
U.S. Sales 2003

Last Name	First Name	Region	Qtr 1	Qtr 2
Arman	Simon	East	$ 14,815.00	$ 13,100.00
Bartholomew	Barbara	North	$ 24,500.00	$ 25,600.00
Childs	Alice	West	$ 20,900.00	$ 22,600.00
	Linda	East	$ 15,900.00	$ 22,700.00
	Sam	North	$ 25,000.00	$ 34,000.00
McTague	Michael	Northwest	$ 24,110.00	$ 54,812.00
Quayle	Antonio	West	$ 25,600.00	$ 48,752.00
Rivena	Orlando	South	$ 22,600.00	$ 58,445.00
Stark	Oscar	Southwest	$ 22,700.00	$ 48,648.00
Unger	Maria	Southwest	$ 23,300.00	$ 24,600.00
Hanover	Caroline	East	$ 23,800.00	$ 27,700.00
Jaen	Enrique	West	$ 54,826.00	$ 598,224.00
Monder	Alana	Southwest	$ 31,200.00	$ 23,100.00
Innoue	Chika	South	$ 50,224.00	$ 17,300.00
Ryan	Maureen	Midwest	$ 15,500.00	$ 10,000.00
Simmonds	Leon	West	$ 30,900.00	$ 24,400.00
Clark	John	East	$ 14,815.00	$ 13,100.00
Rapp	Amanda	North	$ 24,500.00	$ 25,600.00
Booth	Cathy	Northwest	$ 20,900.00	$ 22,600.00
Diehl	Jim	West	$ 15,900.00	$ 22,700.00
Smith	Elizabeth	South	$ 25,000.00	$ 34,000.00
Merkley	Katie	Southwest	$ 24,110.00	$ 54,812.00
Cuzens	Beth	Southwest	$ 25,600.00	$ 48,752.00

Printed Page 1

Qtr 3	Qtr 4	Total
$ 11,580.00	$ 17,300.00	$ 56,795.00
$ 22,000.00	$ 19,000.00	$ 91,100.00
$ 20,140.00	$ 24,400.00	$ 88,040.00
$ 17,600.00	$ 20,000.00	$ 76,200.00
$ 21,000.00	$ 35,000.00	$ 115,000.00
$ 15,200.00	$ 25,600.00	$ 119,722.00
$ 30,300.00	$ 22,600.00	$ 127,252.00
$ 16,800.00	$ 22,700.00	$ 120,545.00
$ 36,855.00	$ 35,000.00	$ 143,203.00
$ 21,380.00	$ 15,937.00	$ 85,217.00
$ 12,600.00	$ 35,000.00	$ 99,100.00
$ 24,100.00	$ 28,000.00	$ 705,150.00
$ 17,700.00	$ 29,300.00	$ 101,300.00
$ 15,200.00	$ 14,600.00	$ 97,324.00
$ 30,300.00	$ 22,600.00	$ 87,400.00
$ 16,800.00	$ 24,513.00	$ 96,613.00
$ 11,580.00	$ 17,300.00	$ 56,795.00
$ 22,000.00	$ 19,000.00	$ 91,100.00
$ 20,140.00	$ 24,400.00	$ 88,040.00
$ 17,600.00	$ 20,000.00	$ 76,200.00
$ 21,000.00	$ 35,000.00	$ 115,000.00
$ 15,200.00	$ 25,600.00	$ 119,722.00
$ 30,300.00	$ 22,600.00	$ 127,252.00

Printed Page 2

Figure 6-9: *A worksheet that appears on two printed pages.*

Benjamin of Brussels
International Chocolate Distributors, Inc.

U.S. Sales 2003

Last Name	First Name	Region	Qtr 1	Qtr 2	Qtr 3	Qtr 4	Total
Arman	Simon	East	$ 14,815.00	$ 13,100.00	$ 11,580.00	$ 17,300.00	$ 56,795.00
Bartholomew	Barbara	North	$ 24,500.00	$ 25,600.00	$ 22,000.00	$ 19,000.00	$ 91,100.00
Childs	Alice	West	$ 20,900.00	$ 22,600.00	$ 20,140.00	$ 24,400.00	$ 88,040.00
Greenburg	Linda	East	$ 15,900.00	$ 22,700.00	$ 17,600.00	$ 20,000.00	$ 76,200.00
Lundquist	Sam	North	$ 25,000.00	$ 34,000.00	$ 21,000.00	$ 35,000.00	$ 115,000.00
McTague	Michael	Northwest	$ 24,110.00	$ 54,812.00	$ 15,200.00	$ 25,600.00	$ 119,722.00
Quayle	Antonio	West	$ 25,600.00	$ 48,752.00	$ 30,300.00	$ 22,600.00	$ 127,252.00
Rivena	Orlando	South	$ 22,600.00	$ 58,445.00	$ 16,800.00	$ 22,700.00	$ 120,545.00
Stark	Oscar	Southwest	$		$ 36,855.00	$ 35,000.00	$ 143,203.00
Unger	Maria	Southwest	$ One Printed Page		$ 21,380.00	$ 15,937.00	$ 85,217.00
Hanover	Caroline	East	$		$ 12,600.00	$ 35,000.00	$ 99,100.00
Jaen	Enrique	West	$ 54,826.00	$ 598,224.00	$ 24,100.00	$ 28,000.00	$ 705,150.00
Monder	Alana	Southwest	$ 31,200.00	$ 23,100.00	$ 17,700.00	$ 29,300.00	$ 101,300.00
Innoue	Chika	South	$ 50,224.00	$ 17,300.00	$ 15,200.00	$ 14,600.00	$ 97,324.00
Ryan	Maureen	Midwest	$ 15,500.00	$ 19,000.00	$ 30,300.00	$ 22,600.00	$ 87,400.00
Simmonds	Leon	West	$ 30,900.00	$ 24,400.00	$ 16,800.00	$ 24,513.00	$ 96,613.00
Clark	John	East	$ 14,815.00	$ 13,100.00	$ 11,580.00	$ 17,300.00	$ 56,795.00
Rapp	Amanda	North	$ 24,500.00	$ 25,600.00	$ 22,000.00	$ 19,000.00	$ 91,100.00
Booth	Cathy	Northwest	$ 20,900.00	$ 22,600.00	$ 20,140.00	$ 24,400.00	$ 88,040.00
Diehl	Jim	West	$ 15,900.00	$ 22,700.00	$ 17,600.00	$ 20,000.00	$ 76,200.00
Smith	Elizabeth	South	$ 25,000.00	$ 34,000.00	$ 21,000.00	$ 35,000.00	$ 115,000.00
Merkley	Katie	Southwest	$ 24,110.00	$ 54,812.00	$ 15,200.00	$ 25,600.00	$ 119,722.00
Cuzens	Beth	Southwest	$ 25,600.00	$ 48,752.00	$ 30,300.00	$ 22,600.00	$ 127,252.00

Figure 6-10: *A worksheet that appears on one printed page.*

By altering the page orientation of a worksheet, you can keep related data together in a logical format.

Page Orientation

Excel provides two types of page orientation. The first, Portrait, displays data with the paper positioned vertically. The other is Landscape, in which the paper is positioned horizontally. You adjust page orientation in the Page Setup dialog box, which is shown in the following figure, Figure 6-11.

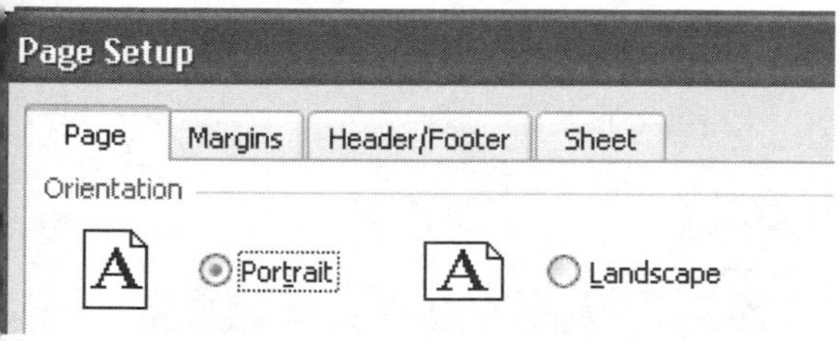

Figure 6-11: *Page orientation options.*

How to Change Page Orientation

Procedure Reference: Change Page Orientation

To change page orientation:

1. Choose File→Page Setup to open the Page Setup dialog box.

2. Click the Page tab.

3. Under Orientation, select either Portrait or Landscape.

4. Click OK to apply the change.

ACTIVITY 6-4

Changing Page Orientation

Objective:

To change page orientation.

Setup:

Activity 6-3 is complete. The file PrintPractice is open.

Scenario:

You are ready to print your document, but when you preview it, you notice that the worksheet data is too wide to fit on the page. You want to change the orientation of your page from Portrait to Landscape to solve this problem.

What You Do	How You Do It
1. **Change the page orientation to Landscape.**	a. **Choose File→Page Setup.**
	b. **Click the Page tab** to view the available options.
	c. In the Orientation region, **select Landscape.**

Orientation

A ○ Portrait   A ⦿ Landscape

	d. **Click OK.**
2. **Preview the print version of the file.**	a. **Choose File→Print Preview** to view the worksheet.
	b. **Click Zoom** to fit the page within the viewable area of the screen.
3. **Print the workbook.**	a. **Click Print** to open the Print dialog box. For the purposes of this course, you will not actually send this file to the printer. If you were going to print it, you would click OK at this point.
	b. **Click Cancel.**

TOPIC E

Insert and Remove Page Breaks

When printing your worksheet, you might want the printed pages to break at specific points. In this topic, you will insert and remove page breaks.

You have a worksheet that stores the sales records for every salesperson in your organization. Which printout better organizes the names of the sales reps, the one shown in Figure 6-12 or the one shown in Figure 6-13?

Last Name	First Name	Region	Qtr 1	Qtr 2	Qtr 3	Qtr 4	Total
Northeast Division							
Arman	Simon	East	$ 14,815.00	$ 13,100.00	$ 11,580.00	$ 17,300.00	$ 56,795.00
Bartholomew	Barbara	North	$ 24,500.00	$ 25,600.00	$ 22,000.00	$ 19,000.00	$ 91,100.00
Childs	Alice	West	$ 20,900.00	$ 22,600.00	$ 20,140.00	$ 24,400.00	$ 88,040.00
Greenburg	Linda	East	$ 15,900.00	$ 22,700.00	$ 17,600.00	$ 20,000.00	$ 76,200.00
Lundquist	Sam	North	$ 25,000.00	$ 34,000.00	$ 21,000.00	$ 35,000.00	$ 115,000.00
McTague	Michael	Northwest	$ 24,110.00	$ 54,812.00	$ 15,200.00	$ 25,600.00	$ 119,722.00
Quayle	Antonio	West	$ 25,600.00	$ 48,752.00	$ 30,300.00	$ 22,600.00	$ 127,252.00
Rivena	Orlando	South	$ 22,600.00	$ 58,445.00	$ 16,800.00	$ 22,700.00	$ 120,545.00
Stark	Oscar	Southwest	$ 22,700.00	$ 48,648.00	$ 36,855.00	$ 35,000.00	$ 143,203.00
Ung		Southwest	$ 23,300.00	$ 24,600.00	$ 21,380.00	$ 15,937.00	$ 85,217.00
Han		East	$ 23,800.00	$ 27,700.00	$ 12,600.00	$ 35,000.00	$ 99,100.00
Jaen	Enrique	West	$ 54,826.00	$ 598,224.00	$ 24,100.00	$ 28,000.00	$ 705,150.00
Northwest Division							
Monder	Alana	Southwest	$ 31,200.00	$ 23,100.00	$ 17,700.00	$ 29,300.00	$ 101,300.00
Innoue	Chika	South	$ 50,224.00	$ 17,300.00	$ 15,200.00	$ 14,600.00	$ 97,324.00
Ryan	Maureen	Midwest	$ 15,500.00	$ 19,000.00	$ 30,300.00	$ 22,600.00	$ 87,400.00
Simmonds	Leon	West	$ 30,900.00	$ 24,400.00	$ 16,800.00	$ 24,513.00	$ 96,613.00
Clark	John	East	$ 14,815.00	$ 13,100.00	$ 11,580.00	$ 17,300.00	$ 56,795.00
Rapp	Amanda	North	$ 24,500.00	$ 25,600.00	$ 22,000.00	$ 19,000.00	$ 91,100.00
Booth	Cathy	Northwest	$ 20,900.00	$ 22,600.00	$ 20,140.00	$ 24,400.00	$ 88,040.00
Diehl	Jim	West	$ 15,900.00	$ 22,700.00	$ 17,600.00	$ 20,000.00	$ 76,200.00
Smith	Elizabeth	South	$ 25,000.00	$ 34,000.00	$ 21,000.00	$ 35,000.00	$ 115,000.00
Merkley	Katie	Southwest	$ 24,110.00	$ 54,812.00	$ 15,200.00	$ 25,600.00	$ 119,722.00
Cuzens	Beth	Southwest	$ 25,600.00	$ 48,752.00	$ 30,300.00	$ 22,600.00	$ 127,252.00

Printed Page 1

Printed Page 2

8 of 8   US Sales 2003   10:02 AM

Last Name	First Name	Region	Qtr 1	Qtr 2	Qtr 3	Qtr 4	Total
Saylor	Rachel	East	$ 22,600.00	$ 58,445.00	$ 16,800.00	$ 22,700.00	$ 120,545.00
Wilson	Tom	West	$ 22,700.00	$ 48,648.00	$ 36,855.00	$ 35,000.00	$ 143,203.00
Hartson	Sue	Southwest	$ 23,300.00	$ 24,600.00	$ 21,380.00	$ 15,937.00	$ 85,217.00
Sandler	Cheryl	South	$ 23,800.00	$ 27,700.00	$ 12,600.00	$ 35,000.00	$ 99,100.00
Silkey	Marilyn	Midwest	$ 54,826.00	$ 75,894.00	$ 24,100.00	$ 28,000.00	$ 182,820.00
Neff	Chris	West	$ 31,200.00	$ 23,100.00	$ 17,700.00	$ 29,300.00	$ 101,300.00
Hyder	Jeff	Southwest	$ 5,623.00	$ 17,300.00	$ 15,200.00	$ 14,600.00	$ 52,723.00
Schwab	Jan	East	$ 15,500.00	$ 19,000.00	$ 30,300.00	$ 22,600.00	$ 87,400.00

Figure 6-12: *A printout with no page breaks.*

Benjamin of Brussels
International Chocolate Distributors, Inc.
U.S. Sales 2003

Last Name	First Name	Region	Qtr 1	Qtr 2	Qtr 3	Qtr 4	Total
Northeast Division							
Arman	Simon	East	$ 14,815.00	$ 13,100.00	$ 11,580.00	$ 17,300.00	$ 56,795.00
Bartholomew	Barbara	North	$ 24,500.00	$ 25,600.00	$ 22,000.00	$ 19,000.00	$ 91,100.00
Childs	Alice	West	$ 20,900.00	$ 22,600.00	$ 20,140.00	$ 24,400.00	$ 88,040.00
Printed Page 1		East	$ 15,900.00	$ 22,700.00	$ 17,600.00	$ 20,000.00	$ 76,200.00
		North	$ 25,000.00	$ 34,000.00	$ 21,000.00	$ 35,000.00	$ 115,000.00
McTague	Michael	Northwest	$ 24,110.00	$ 54,812.00	$ 15,200.00	$ 25,600.00	$ 119,722.00
Quayle	Antonio	West	$ 25,600.00	$ 48,752.00	$ 30,300.00	$ 22,600.00	$ 127,252.00
Rivena	Orlando	South	$ 22,600.00	$ 58,445.00	$ 16,800.00	$ 22,700.00	$ 120,545.00
Stark	Oscar	Southwest	$ 22,700.00	$ 48,648.00	$ 36,855.00	$ 35,000.00	$ 143,203.00
Unger	Maria	Southwest	$ 23,300.00	$ 24,600.00	$ 21,380.00	$ 15,937.00	$ 85,217.00
Hanover	Caroline	East	$ 23,800.00	$ 27,700.00	$ 12,600.00	$ 35,000.00	$ 99,100.00
Jaen	Enrique	West	$ 54,826.00	$ 598,224.00	$ 24,100.00	$ 28,000.00	$ 705,150.00

Last Name	First Name	Region	Qtr 1	Qtr 2	Qtr 3	Qtr 4	Total
Northwest Division							
Monder	Alana	Southwest	$ 31,200.00	$ 23,100.00	$ 17,700.00	$ 29,300.00	$ 101,300.00
Innoue	Chika	South	$ 50,224.00	$ 17,300.00	$ 15,200.00	$ 14,600.00	$ 97,324.00
Ryan	Maureen	Midwest	$ 15,500.00	$ 19,000.00	$ 30,300.00	$ 22,600.00	$ 87,400.00
Simmonds	Leon	West	$ 30,900.00	$ 24,400.00	$ 16,800.00	$ 24,513.00	$ 96,613.00
Clark	John	East	$ 14,815.00	$ 13,100.00	$ 11,580.00	$ 17,300.00	$ 56,795.00
Rapp	Amanda	North	$ 24,500.00	$ 25,600.00	$ 22,000.00	$ 19,000.00	$ 91,100.00
Booth	Cathy	Northwest	$ 20,900.00	$ 22,600.00	$ 20,140.00	$ 24,400.00	$ 88,040.00
Diehl	Jim	West	$ 15,900.00	$ 22,700.00	$ 17,600.00	$ 20,000.00	$ 76,200.00
Smith	Elizabeth	South	$ 25,000.00	$ 34,000.00	$ 21,000.00	$ 35,000.00	$ 115,000.00
Markley	Katie	Southwest	$ 24,110.00	$ 54,812.00	$ 15,200.00	$ 25,600.00	$ 119,722.00
Printed Page 2		Southwest	$ 25,600.00	$ 48,752.00	$ 30,300.00	$ 22,600.00	$ 127,252.00
		East	$ 22,600.00	$ 58,445.00	$ 16,800.00	$ 22,700.00	$ 120,545.00
Wilson	Tom	West	$ 22,700.00	$ 48,648.00	$ 36,855.00	$ 35,000.00	$ 143,203.00
Hartson	Sue	Southwest	$ 23,300.00	$ 24,600.00	$ 21,380.00	$ 15,937.00	$ 85,217.00
Sandler	Cheryl	South	$ 23,800.00	$ 27,700.00	$ 12,600.00	$ 35,000.00	$ 99,100.00
Silkey	Marilyn	Midwest	$ 54,826.00	$ 75,894.00	$ 24,100.00	$ 28,000.00	$ 182,820.00
Neff	Chris	West	$ 31,200.00	$ 23,100.00	$ 17,700.00	$ 29,300.00	$ 101,300.00
Hyder	Jeff	Southwest	$ 5,623.00	$ 17,300.00	$ 15,200.00	$ 14,600.00	$ 52,723.00
Schwab	Jan	East	$ 15,500.00	$ 19,000.00	$ 30,300.00	$ 22,600.00	$ 87,400.00

Figure 6-13: *A printout with page breaks.*

Adding page breaks to a worksheet prior to printing helps keep related information together on the printout.

Page Breaks

When a worksheet printout is too large to fit on one piece of paper, vertically or horizontally, Excel breaks the printout into multiple pages. If you do not like where the automatic page breaks separate your data, you can manually insert your own page breaks.

How to Insert and Remove Page Breaks

Procedure Reference: Insert Page Breaks

To insert a page break:

1. Select the row or column that will be the first row or column on the new page.

2. Choose Insert→Page Break to insert the page break.

Procedure Reference: Remove Page Breaks

To remove a page break:

1. Select the column immediately to the right of the page break or the row immediately below the page break.

2. Choose Insert→Remove Page Break to remove the page break.

ACTIVITY 6-5

Inserting and Removing Page Breaks

Objective:
To insert and remove page breaks.

Setup:
Activity 6-4 is complete. The file PrintPractice is open.

Scenario:
You have a worksheet that has multiple pages. The only problem is that the pages are breaking in places that you don't want them to, separating data that really needs to stay together. By inserting your own page breaks, you can control where the pages are broken.

What You Do	How You Do It
1. Insert a page break before row 28.	a. Click the row 28 row heading.
	b. Choose Insert→Page Break to insert a page break above row 28.
2. Preview the print version of the file.	a. Choose File→Print Preview to view the worksheet.
	b. Click Page Break Preview to preview the page breaks.
	c. In the Welcome To Page Break Preview dialog box, check the Do Not Show This Dialog Again check box, and then click OK to view the page breaks in the file.
	d. Choose View→Normal to revert back to the normal view.

3. Delete the page break you added before row 28, insert a new page break after row 21, and then save your work.

a. **Choose Insert→Remove Page Break** to remove the page break that you inserted before row 28.

b. **Choose File→Print Preview** to view the worksheet.

c. **Click Page Break Preview** to preview the page breaks.

d. **Drag the blue hash line up to the line immediately below row 21.**

e. **Choose View→Normal** to revert back to the normal view.

f. **Click the Save button.**

TOPIC F

Print a Range

When printing a worksheet, you might want to print a specific subset of data. In this topic, you will print a range.

You have a long worksheet that contains data on sales associates. Your manager needs a printout, but she only wants to see the data for sales associates whose last names begin with the letter "C." Which printout would better serve your manager's needs, the one shown in Figure 6-14 or the one shown in Figure 6-15?

Last Name	First Name	Region	Qtr 1	Qtr 2	Qtr 3	Qtr 4	Total
Arman	Simon	East	$ 14,815.00	$ 13,100.00	$ 11,580.00	$ 17,300.00	$ 56,795.00
Bartholomew	Barbara	North	$ 24,500.00	$ 25,600.00	$ 22,000.00	$ 19,000.00	$ 91,100.00
Booth	Cathy	Northwest	$ 20,900.00	$ 22,600.00	$ 20,140.00	$ 24,400.00	$ 88,040.00
Chaffee	Angela	Midwest	$ 24,110.00	$ 54,812.00	$ 15,200.00	$ 25,600.00	$ 119,722.00
Chan	Caryl	Midwest	$ 22,700.00	$ 48,648.00	$ 36,855.00	$ 35,000.00	$ 143,203.00
Childs	Alice	West	$ 20,900.00	$ 22,600.00	$ 20,140.00	$ 24,400.00	$ 88,040.00
Clark	John	East	$ 14,815.00	$ 13,100.00	$ 11,580.00	$ 17,300.00	$ 56,795.00
Cuzens	Beth	Southwest	$ 25,600.00	$ 48,752.00	$ 30,300.00	$ 22,600.00	$ 127,252.00
Decker	Janet	Southwest	$ 15,900.00	$ 22,700.00	$ 17,600.00	$ 20,000.00	$ 76,200.00
Diehl	Jim	West	$ 15,900.00	$ 22,700.00	$ 17,600.00	$ 20,000.00	$ 76,200.00
Foster	Christine	Southwest	$ 14,815.00	$ 13,100.00	$ 11,580.00	$ 17,300.00	$ 56,795.00
French	Frank	Southwest	$ 31,200.00	$ 12,447.00	$ 17,700.00	$ 29,300.00	$ 90,647.00
Greenburg	Linda	East	$ 15,900.00	$ 22,700.00	$ 17,600.00	$ 20,000.00	$ 76,200.00
Greenburg	Gail	Southwest	$ 22,600.00	$ 58,445.00	$ 16,800.00	$ 22,700.00	$ 120,545.00
Hack	Greg	East	$ 23,800.00	$ 27,700.00	$ 12,600.00	$ 35,000.00	$ 99,100.00
Hanover	Caroline	East	$ 23,800.00	$ 27,700.00	$ 12,600.00	$ 35,000.00	$ 99,100.00
Hartman	Bob	West	$ 54,826.00	$ 88,743.00	$ 24,100.00	$ 28,000.00	$ 195,669.00
Hartson	Sue	Southwest	$ 23,300.00	$ 24,600.00	$ 21,380.00	$ 15,937.00	$ 85,217.00
Huntt	Marcia	West	$ 30,900.00	$ 24,400.00	$ 16,800.00	$ 24,513.00	$ 96,613.00
Hurley	Arica	South	$ 25,000.00	$ 34,000.00	$ 21,000.00	$ 35,000.00	$ 115,000.00
Hyder	Jeff	Southwest	$ 5,623.00	$ 17,300.00	$ 15,200.00	$ 14,600.00	$ 52,723.00
Innoue	Chika	South	$ 50,224.00	$ 17,300.00	$ 15,200.00	$ 14,600.00	$ 97,324.00
Jaen	Enrique	West	$ 54,826.00	$ 598,224.00	$ 24,100.00	$ 28,000.00	$ 705,150.00

Figure 6-14: *A printout with the requested sales associates noted.*

B of B   US Sales 2003   10:12 AM

Last Name	First Name	Region	Qtr 1	Qtr 2	Qtr 3	Qtr 4	Total
Chaffee	Angela	Midwest	$ 24,110.00	$ 54,812.00	$ 15,200.00	$ 25,600.00	$ 119,722.00
Chan	Caryl	Midwest	$ 22,700.00	$ 48,648.00	$ 36,855.00	$ 35,000.00	$ 143,203.00
Childs	Alice	West	$ 20,900.00	$ 22,600.00	$ 20,140.00	$ 24,400.00	$ 88,040.00
Clark	John	East	$ 14,815.00	$ 13,100.00	$ 11,580.00	$ 17,300.00	$ 56,795.00
Cuzens	Beth	Southwest	$ 25,600.00	$ 48,752.00	$ 30,300.00	$ 22,600.00	$ 127,252.00

Figure 6-15: *A printout of only the requested data.*

Printing a range saves paper when only small subsets of a worksheet are needed. It also aids readers of the printout because they only have to read the data important to their current situation, rather than sift through extraneous data they don't need to read.

How to Print a Range

Procedure Reference: Print a Range

To print a range:

1. Select the range of cells you want to print.

2. Choose File→Print.

3. Under Print What, select Selection.

4. Click OK to print the range.

ACTIVITY 6-6

Printing a Range

Objective:

To print a range.

Setup:

Activity 6-5 is complete. The file PrintPractice is open.

Scenario:

You are about to attend a meeting with people on your development team who need to see some of the information on the PrintPractice worksheet. However, they don't need all of the information; they only need to see the first 10 rows of the worksheet. You have decided to select that range of cells and print them, rather than print the entire worksheet.

What You Do	How You Do It
1. Select cells A1 through H10.	a. Select cell H10.
	b. Press and hold Shift, and then click cell A1 to select the range.
2. Preview the printable range.	a. Choose File→Print to open the Print dialog box.
	b. In the Print What region of the Print dialog box, **select Selection**.

	c. Click Preview to preview the printable region.

	d. Click Close to revert back to the normal view.

3. Print the range and close the file.

a. Choose File→Print to open the Print dialog box.

b. In the Print What region, **select Selection.** For the purposes of this course, you will not actually send this file to the printer. If you were going to print it, you would click OK at this point.

c. **Click Cancel.**

d. **Close the file.**

Lesson 6 Follow-up

In this lesson, you printed the contents of a workbook. Printing allows you to distribute your workbooks when it's not feasible to distribute them electronically.

1. **What are some of the various things you can do to prepare a workbook for printing?**

2. **Based on your knowledge of Excel, what are some reasons you might have to print a workbook?**

NOTES

LESSON 7
Customizing Layout

Lesson Time
45 minutes

Lesson Objectives:

In this lesson, you will customize the layout of the Excel window.

You will:

*   Split a worksheet.
*   Arrange worksheets.
*   Freeze and unfreeze rows and columns.
*   Hide and unhide worksheets.

Introduction

As you continue working in Excel, you will want to start customizing the way you view Excel data while you are working in the application. In this lesson, you will customize the layout of the Excel application window.

The following figure, Figure 7-1, shows a worksheet with multiple columns.

	A	B	C	D	E	F	G	H	I	J	
1					Benjamin of Brussels						
					International Chocolate Distributors, Inc.						
2											
3						2002 Sales				2003 Sales	
4	Last Name	First Name	Region	Qtr 1	Qtr 2	Qtr 3	Qtr 4	Qtr 1	Qtr 2	Qtr 3	Qtr 4
5	Arman	Simon	East	$ 14,815.00	$ 13,100.00	$ 11,580.00	$ 17,300.00	$ 14,815.00	$ 13,100.00	$ 11,580.00	$
6	Bartholomew	Barbara	North	$ 24,500.00	$ 25,600.00	$ 22,000.00	$ 19,000.00	$ 24,500.00	$ 25,600.00	$ 22,000.00	$
7	Childs	Alice	West	$ 20,900.00	$ 22,600.00	$ 20,140.00	$ 24,400.00	$ 20,900.00	$ 22,600.00	$ 20,140.00	$
8	Greenburg	Linda	East	$ 15,900.00	$ 22,700.00	$ 17,600.00	$ 20,000.00	$ 15,900.00	$ 22,700.00	$ 17,600.00	$
9	Lundquist	Sam	North	$ 25,000.00	$ 34,000.00	$ 21,000.00	$ 35,000.00	$ 25,000.00	$ 34,000.00	$ 21,000.00	$:
10	McTague	Michael	Northwest	$ 24,110.00	$ 54,812.00	$ 15,200.00	$ 25,600.00	$ 24,110.00	$ 54,812.00	$ 15,200.00	$:
11	Quayle	Antonio	West	$ 25,600.00	$ 48,752.00	$ 30,300.00	$ 22,600.00	$ 25,600.00	$ 48,752.00	$ 30,300.00	$:
12	Rivena	Orlando	South	$ 22,600.00	$ 58,445.00	$ 16,800.00	$ 22,700.00	$ 22,600.00	$ 58,445.00	$ 16,800.00	$:
13	Stark	Oscar	Southwest	$ 22,700.00	$ 48,648.00	$ 36,855.00	$ 35,000.00	$ 22,700.00	$ 48,648.00	$ 36,855.00	$:
14	Unger	Maria	Southwest	$ 23,300.00	$ 24,600.00	$ 21,380.00	$ 15,937.00	$ 23,300.00	$ 24,600.00	$ 21,380.00	$:
15	Hanover	Caroline	East	$ 23,800.00	$ 27,700.00	$ 12,600.00	$ 35,000.00	$ 23,800.00	$ 27,700.00	$ 12,600.00	$:
16	Jaen	Enrique	West	$ 54,826.00	$598,224.00	$ 24,100.00	$ 28,000.00	$ 54,826.00	598,224.00	$ 24,100.00	$:
17	Monder	Alana	Southwest	$ 31,200.00	$ 23,100.00	$ 17,700.00	$ 29,300.00	$ 31,200.00	$ 23,100.00	$ 17,700.00	$:
18	Innoue	Chika	South	$ 50,224.00	$ 17,300.00	$ 15,200.00	$ 14,600.00	$ 50,224.00	$ 17,300.00	$ 15,200.00	$:
19	Ryan	Maureen	Midwest	$ 15,500.00	$ 19,000.00	$ 30,300.00	$ 22,600.00	$ 15,500.00	$ 19,000.00	$ 30,300.00	$:
20	Simmonds	Leon	West	$ 30,900.00	$ 24,400.00	$ 16,800.00	$ 24,513.00	$ 30,900.00	$ 24,400.00	$ 16,800.00	$:
21	Clark	John	East	$ 14,815.00	$ 13,100.00	$ 11,580.00	$ 17,300.00	$ 14,815.00	$ 13,100.00	$ 11,580.00	$:
22	Rapp	Amanda	North	$ 24,500.00	$ 25,600.00	$ 22,000.00	$ 19,000.00	$ 24,500.00	$ 25,600.00	$ 22,000.00	$:
23	Booth	Cathy	Northwest	$ 20,900.00	$ 22,600.00	$ 20,140.00	$ 24,400.00	$ 20,900.00	$ 22,600.00	$ 20,140.00	$:
24	Diehl	Jim	West	$ 15,900.00	$ 22,700.00	$ 17,600.00	$ 20,000.00	$ 15,900.00	$ 22,700.00	$ 17,600.00	$:
25	Smith	Elizabeth	South	$ 25,000.00	$ 34,000.00	$ 21,000.00	$ 35,000.00	$ 25,000.00	$ 34,000.00	$ 21,000.00	$:
26	Merkley	Katie	Southwest	$ 24,110.00	$ 54,812.00	$ 15,200.00	$ 25,600.00	$ 24,110.00	$ 54,812.00	$ 15,200.00	$:
27	Cuzens	Beth	Southwest	$ 25,600.00	$ 48,752.00	$ 30,300.00	$ 22,600.00	$ 25,600.00	$ 48,752.00	$ 30,300.00	$:
28	Saylor	Rachel	East	$ 22,600.00	$ 58,445.00	$ 16,800.00	$ 22,700.00	$ 22,600.00	$ 58,445.00	$ 16,800.00	$:
29	Wilson	Tom	West	$ 22,700.00	$ 48,648.00	$ 36,855.00	$ 35,000.00	$ 22,700.00	$ 48,648.00	$ 36,855.00	$:
30	Hartson	Sue	Southwest	$ 23,300.00	$ 24,600.00	$ 21,380.00	$ 15,937.00	$ 23,300.00	$ 24,600.00	$ 21,380.00	$:
31	Sandler	Cheryl	South	$ 23,800.00	$ 27,700.00	$ 12,600.00	$ 35,000.00	$ 23,800.00	$ 27,700.00	$ 12,600.00	$:

Figure 7-1: *Excel application window with no custom layout.*

You need to view the contents of the first column and the last column side-by-side, as shown in Figure 7-2.

	A	L	M	N	O	P	Q	R	S	T	U	V
4	Last Name	Total										
16	Jaen	$ 1,410,300.00										
17	Monder	$ 202,600.00										
18	Innoue	$ 194,648.00										
19	Ryan	$ 174,800.00										
20	Simmonds	$ 193,226.00										
21	Clark	$ 113,590.00										
22	Rapp	$ 182,200.00										
23	Booth	$ 176,080.00										
24	Diehl	$ 152,400.00										
25	Smith	$ 230,000.00										
26	Merkley	$ 239,444.00										
27	Cuzens	$ 254,504.00										
28	Saylor	$ 241,090.00										
29	Wilson	$ 286,406.00										
30	Hartson	$ 170,434.00										
31	Sandler	$ 198,200.00										
32	Silkey	$ 365,640.00										
33	Neff	$ 202,600.00										
34	Hyder	$ 105,446.00										
35	Schwab	$ 174,800.00										
36	Huntt	$ 193,226.00										
37	Mosher	$ 254,504.00										
38	Watts	$ 241,090.00										
39	Chan	$ 286,406.00										
40	Turk	$ 170,434.00										
41	Hack	$ 198,200.00										
42	Hartman	$ 391,338.00										
43	French	$ 181,294.00										
44	Miller	$ 268,870.00										
45	Ryan	$ 174,800.00										
46	Steif	$ 193,226.00										
47	Foster	$ 113,590.00										
48	Russo	$ 182,200.00										

Figure 7-2: *Excel application window with custom layout.*

You can do this by customizing the layout of the Excel application window.

TOPIC A

Split a Worksheet

One of the ways you can customize a layout is by enabling non-adjacent elements of the worksheet to be viewed together. In this topic, you will split a worksheet.

The following figure, Figure 7-3, shows a worksheet that contains sales data.

	A	B	C	D	E	F	G	H	I	J
1					**Benjamin of Brussels**					
					International Chocolate Distributors, Inc.					
2										
3					**2002 Sales**				**2003 Sales**	
4	**Last Name**	**First Name**	**Region**	**Qtr 1**	**Qtr 2**	**Qtr 3**	**Qtr 4**	**Qtr 1**	**Qtr 2**	**Qtr 3**	**Qtr 4**
5	Arman	Simon	East	$ 14,815.00	$ 13,100.00	$ 11,580.00	$ 17,300.00	$ 14,815.00	$ 13,100.00	$ 11,580.00	$
6	Bartholomew	Barbara	North	$ 24,500.00	$ 25,600.00	$ 22,000.00	$ 19,000.00	$ 24,500.00	$ 25,600.00	$ 22,000.00	$
7	Childs	Alice	West	$ 20,900.00	$ 22,600.00	$ 20,140.00	$ 24,400.00	$ 20,900.00	$ 22,600.00	$ 20,140.00	$
8	Greenburg	Linda	East	$ 15,900.00	$ 22,700.00	$ 17,600.00	$ 20,000.00	$ 15,900.00	$ 22,700.00	$ 17,600.00	$
9	Lundquist	Sam	North	$ 25,000.00	$ 34,000.00	$ 21,000.00	$ 35,000.00	$ 25,000.00	$ 34,000.00	$ 21,000.00	$
10	McTague	Michael	Northwest	$ 24,110.00	$ 54,812.00	$ 15,200.00	$ 25,600.00	$ 24,110.00	$ 54,812.00	$ 15,200.00	$
11	Quayle	Antonio	West	$ 25,600.00	$ 48,752.00	$ 30,300.00	$ 22,600.00	$ 25,600.00	$ 48,752.00	$ 30,300.00	$
12	Rivena	Orlando	South	$ 22,600.00	$ 58,445.00	$ 16,800.00	$ 22,700.00	$ 22,600.00	$ 58,445.00	$ 16,800.00	$
13	Stark	Oscar	Southwest	$ 22,700.00	$ 48,648.00	$ 36,855.00	$ 35,000.00	$ 22,700.00	$ 48,648.00	$ 36,855.00	$
14	Unger	Maria	Southwest	$ 23,300.00	$ 24,600.00	$ 21,380.00	$ 15,937.00	$ 23,300.00	$ 24,600.00	$ 21,380.00	$
15	Hanover	Caroline	East	$ 23,800.00	$ 27,700.00	$ 12,600.00	$ 35,000.00	$ 23,800.00	$ 27,700.00	$ 12,600.00	$
16	Jaen	Enrique	West	$ 54,826.00	$598,224.00	$ 24,100.00	$ 28,000.00	$ 54,826.00	$ 598,224.00	$ 24,100.00	$
17	Monder	Alana	Southwest	$ 31,200.00	$ 23,100.00	$ 17,700.00	$ 29,300.00	$ 31,200.00	$ 23,100.00	$ 17,700.00	$
18	Innoue	Chika	South	$ 50,224.00	$ 17,300.00	$ 15,200.00	$ 14,600.00	$ 50,224.00	$ 17,300.00	$ 15,200.00	$
19	Ryan	Maureen	Midwest	$ 15,500.00	$ 19,000.00	$ 30,300.00	$ 22,600.00	$ 15,500.00	$ 19,000.00	$ 30,300.00	$
20	Simmonds	Leon	West	$ 30,900.00	$ 24,400.00	$ 16,800.00	$ 24,513.00	$ 30,900.00	$ 24,400.00	$ 16,800.00	$
21	Clark	John	East	$ 14,815.00	$ 13,100.00	$ 11,580.00	$ 17,300.00	$ 14,815.00	$ 13,100.00	$ 11,580.00	$
22	Rapp	Amanda	North	$ 24,500.00	$ 25,600.00	$ 22,000.00	$ 19,000.00	$ 24,500.00	$ 25,600.00	$ 22,000.00	$
23	Booth	Cathy	Northwest	$ 20,900.00	$ 22,600.00	$ 20,140.00	$ 24,400.00	$ 20,900.00	$ 22,600.00	$ 20,140.00	$
24	Diehl	Jim	West	$ 15,900.00	$ 22,700.00	$ 17,600.00	$ 20,000.00	$ 15,900.00	$ 22,700.00	$ 17,600.00	$
25	Smith	Elizabeth	South	$ 25,000.00	$ 34,000.00	$ 21,000.00	$ 35,000.00	$ 25,000.00	$ 34,000.00	$ 21,000.00	$
26	Merkley	Katie	Southwest	$ 24,110.00	$ 54,812.00	$ 15,200.00	$ 25,600.00	$ 24,110.00	$ 54,812.00	$ 15,200.00	$
27	Cuzens	Beth	Southwest	$ 25,600.00	$ 48,752.00	$ 30,300.00	$ 22,600.00	$ 25,600.00	$ 48,752.00	$ 30,300.00	$
28	Saylor	Rachel	East	$ 22,600.00	$ 58,445.00	$ 16,800.00	$ 22,700.00	$ 22,600.00	$ 58,445.00	$ 16,800.00	$
29	Wilson	Tom	West	$ 22,700.00	$ 48,648.00	$ 36,855.00	$ 35,000.00	$ 22,700.00	$ 48,648.00	$ 36,855.00	$
30	Hartson	Sue	Southwest	$ 23,300.00	$ 24,600.00	$ 21,380.00	$ 15,937.00	$ 23,300.00	$ 24,600.00	$ 21,380.00	$
31	Sandler	Cheryl	South	$ 23,800.00	$ 27,700.00	$ 12,600.00	$ 35,000.00	$ 23,800.00	$ 27,700.00	$ 12,600.00	$
32	Silkey	Marilyn	Midwest	$ 54,826.00	$ 75,894.00	$ 24,100.00	$ 28,000.00	$ 54,826.00	$ 75,894.00	$ 24,100.00	$

Figure 7-3: *A worksheet with no split.*

If you want to compare the Qtr 1 sales totals to the Qtr 4 sales totals, would it be easier to scroll horizontally between both of the those columns or view the columns side-by-side, as shown in Figure 7-4?

	A	B	H	I	J	K	L	M	N
3					**2003 Sales**				
4	**Last Name**	**First Name**	**Qtr 1**	**Qtr 2**	**Qtr 3**	**Qtr 4**	**Total Sales for 2002 and 2003**		
5	Arman	Simon	$ 14,815.00	$ 13,100.00	$ 11,580.00	$ 17,300.00	$		113,590.00
6	Bartholomew	Barbara	$ 24,500.00	$ 25,600.00	$ 22,000.00	$ 19,000.00	$		182,200.00
7	Childs	Alice	$ 20,900.00	$ 22,600.00	$ 20,140.00	$ 24,400.00	$		176,080.00
8	Greenburg	Linda	$ 15,900.00	$ 22,700.00	$ 17,600.00	$ 20,000.00	$		152,400.00
9	Lundquist	Sam	$ 25,000.00	$ 34,000.00	$ 21,000.00	$ 35,000.00	$		230,000.00
10	McTague	Michael	$ 24,110.00	$ 54,812.00	$ 15,200.00	$ 25,600.00	$		239,444.00
11	Quayle	Antonio	$ 25,600.00	$ 48,752.00	$ 30,300.00	$ 22,600.00	$		254,504.00
12	Rivena	Orlando	$ 22,600.00	$ 58,445.00	$ 16,800.00	$ 22,700.00	$		241,090.00
13	Stark	Oscar	$ 22,700.00	$ 48,648.00	$ 36,855.00	$ 35,000.00	$		286,406.00
14	Unger	Maria	$ 23,300.00	$ 24,600.00	$ 21,380.00	$ 15,937.00	$		170,434.00
15	Hanover	Caroline	$ 23,800.00	$ 27,700.00	$ 12,600.00	$ 35,000.00	$		198,200.00
16	Jaen	Enrique	$ 54,826.00	$ 98,224.00	$ 24,100.00	$ 28,000.00	$		910,300.00
17	Monder	Alana	$ 31,200.00	$ 23,100.00	$ 17,700.00	$ 29,300.00	$		202,600.00
18	Innoue	Chika	$ 50,224.00	$ 17,300.00	$ 15,200.00	$ 14,600.00	$		194,648.00
19	Ryan	Maureen	$ 15,500.00	$ 19,000.00	$ 30,300.00	$ 22,600.00	$		174,800.00
20	Simmonds	Leon	$ 30,900.00	$ 24,400.00	$ 16,800.00	$ 24,513.00	$		193,226.00
21	Clark	John	$ 14,815.00	$ 13,100.00	$ 11,580.00	$ 17,300.00	$		113,590.00
22	Rapp	Amanda	$ 24,500.00	$ 25,600.00	$ 22,000.00	$ 19,000.00	$		182,200.00
23	Booth	Cathy	$ 20,900.00	$ 22,600.00	$ 20,140.00	$ 24,400.00	$		176,080.00
24	Diehl	Jim	$ 15,900.00	$ 22,700.00	$ 17,600.00	$ 20,000.00	$		152,400.00
25	Smith	Elizabeth	$ 25,000.00	$ 34,000.00	$ 21,000.00	$ 35,000.00	$		230,000.00
26	Merkley	Katie	$ 24,110.00	$ 54,812.00	$ 15,200.00	$ 25,600.00	$		239,444.00
27	Cuzens	Beth	$ 25,600.00	$ 48,752.00	$ 30,300.00	$ 22,600.00	$		254,504.00
28	Saylor	Rachel	$ 22,600.00	$ 58,445.00	$ 16,800.00	$ 22,700.00	$		241,090.00

Figure 7-4: *A worksheet with a split.*

Splitting a worksheet allows you to view specific elements of the worksheet on-screen at the same time.

How to Split a Worksheet

Procedure Reference: Split a Worksheet

To split a worksheet:

1. Select any cell in the center of the worksheet you want to split.

2. Choose Window→Split to add the split bars to the worksheet.

3. Drag the split bars as needed to split the worksheet.

ACTIVITY 7-1

Splitting a Worksheet

Objective:

To split a worksheet.

Setup:

The file PrintPractice is open.

Scenario:

You are in the process of reviewing the data you've entered in the PrintPractice worksheet. Because there are so many names and numbers on the sheet, it's getting difficult to keep your focus on the data you want to read. You want to read the contents of the Qtr 4 column and confirm that the column contains the correct data. To help make this easier, you've decided to split the worksheet so that you can view the Last Name column heading in one view, the Qtr 4 and Total column headings in another view, the employee last names in a third view, and the values for the Qtr 4 and Total columns in a fourth view, as shown in Figure 7-5.

	A	G	H	I
4	**Last Name**	**Qtr 4**	**Total**	
5	Arman	$ 17,300.00	$ 56,795.00	
6	Bartholomew	$ 19,000.00	$ 91,100.00	
7	Childs	$ 24,400.00	$ 88,040.00	
8	Greenburg	$ 20,000.00	$ 76,200.00	
9	Lundquist	$ 35,000.00	$ 115,000.00	
10	McTague	$ 25,600.00	$ 119,722.00	
11	Quayle	$ 22,600.00	$ 127,252.00	
12	Rivena	$ 22,700.00	$ 120,545.00	
13	Stark	$ 35,000.00	$ 143,203.00	
14	Unger	$ 15,937.00	$ 85,217.00	
15	Hanover	$ 35,000.00	$ 99,100.00	

Figure 7-5: *A split worksheet.*

What You Do	How You Do It
1. Apply a split view to the worksheet.	a. **Select cell E15** to place the insertion point in the center of the worksheet.

b. **Choose Window→Split** to add the split lines to the view.

Region	Qtr 1	Qtr 2	Qtr 3	Qtr 4
East	$ 14,815.00	$ 13,100.00	$ 11,580.00	$ 17
North	$ 24,500.00	$ 25,600.00	$ 22,000.00	$ 19
West	$ 20,900.00	$ 22,600.00	$ 20,140.00	$ 24
East	$ 15,900.00	$ 22,700.00	$ 17,600.00	$ 20
North	$ 25,000.00	$ 34,000.00	$ 21,000.00	$ 35
Northwest	$ 24,110.00	$ 54,812.00	$ 15,200.00	$ 25
West	$ 25,600.00	$ 48,752.00	$ 30,300.00	$ 22
South	$ 22,600.00	$ 58,445.00	$ 16,800.00	$ 22
Southwest	$ 22,700.00	$ 48,648.00	$ 36,855.00	$ 35
Southwest	$ 23,300.00	$ 24,600.00	$ 21,380.00	$ 15
East	$ 23,800.00	$ 27,700.00	$ 12,600.00	$ 35
West	$ 54,826.00	$ 598,224.00	$ 24,100.00	$ 28
Southwest	$ 31,200.00	$ 23,100.00	$ 17,700.00	$ 29
South	$ 50,224.00	$ 17,300.00	$ 15,200.00	$ 14
Midwest	$ 15,500.00	$ 19,000.00	$ 30,300.00	$ 22
West	$ 30,900.00	$ 24,400.00	$ 16,800.00	$ 24
East	$ 14,815.00	$ 13,100.00	$ 11,580.00	$ 17
North	$ 24,500.00	$ 25,600.00	$ 22,000.00	$ 19
Northwest	$ 20,900.00	$ 22,600.00	$ 20,140.00	$ 24

2. **Place the Last Name column heading in the first quadrant.**

a. Using the top vertical scroll bar, **click the downward scroll arrow until row 4 appears at the top edge of the viewable region.**

b. **Drag the horizontal split up** until only row 4 appears in quadrants 1 and 2.

	A	B	C	D	E	
4	Last Name	First Name	Region	Qtr 1	Qtr 2	Qtr 3
15	Hanover	Caroline	East	$ 23,800.00	$ 27,700.00	$
16	Jaen	Enrique	West	$ 54,826.00	$ 598,224.00	$

c. **Drag the vertical split to the left** until only column A appears in quadrants 1 and 3.

	A	E	F
4	**Last Name**	Qtr 2	Qtr 3
15	Hanover	$ 27,700.00	$ 12,6
16	Jaen	$ 598,224.00	$ 24,1
17	Monder	$ 23,100.00	$ 17,7
18	Innoue	$ 17,300.00	$ 15,2
19	Ryan	$ 19,000.00	$ 30,3

3. Place the Qtr 4 and Total columns' values in the fourth quadrant.

a. Using the right horizontal scroll bar, **click the right pointing scroll arrow until quadrant 2 contains only the Qtr 4 and Total columns.**

	A	G	H	I
4	Last Name	Qtr 4	Total	
15	Hanover	$ 35,000.00	$ 99,100.00	
16	Jaen	$ 28,000.00	$ 705,150.00	
17	Monder	$ 29,300.00	$ 101,300.00	

b. **Click in any empty cell** to deselect any selected cells.

TOPIC B

Arrange Worksheets

You have split a single worksheet to view specific elements of the worksheet on-screen at the same time. Now, you have more than one worksheet in the same workbook that contains data you would like to view on-screen at the same time. In this topic, you will arrange worksheets.

The following figure, Figure 7-6, shows a workbook with multiple worksheets.

	A	B	C	D	E	F	G	H	I	J	K	L
1	**European Division**											
2												
3	Item	QTR 1	QTR 2	QTR 3	QTR 4							
4	Hardware	400	800	900	300							
5	Software	200	500	1200	100							
6	Furniture	300	400	1400	300							
7	Accessories	100	300	500	300							
8												
9	*Totals:*	$1,000	$2,000	$4,000	$1,000							
10												
11												
12												
13												
14												
15												
16												
17												
18												
19												
20												
21												
22												
23												
24												
25												
26												
27												
28												
29												
30												
31												
32												
33												
34												
35												

◄ ◄ ► ►◄ \ Summary \ **European Division** / N American Division / C American Division / Australian Division / Sheet2 / Sheet1 /

Figure 7-6: *A workbook with multiple worksheets.*

If you want to compare the data on the European Division sheet, the N American Division sheet, and the C American Division sheet, would it be easier to click back and forth among all of those worksheets, or view the important elements of each worksheet side-by-side in a single window, as shown in Figure 7-7?

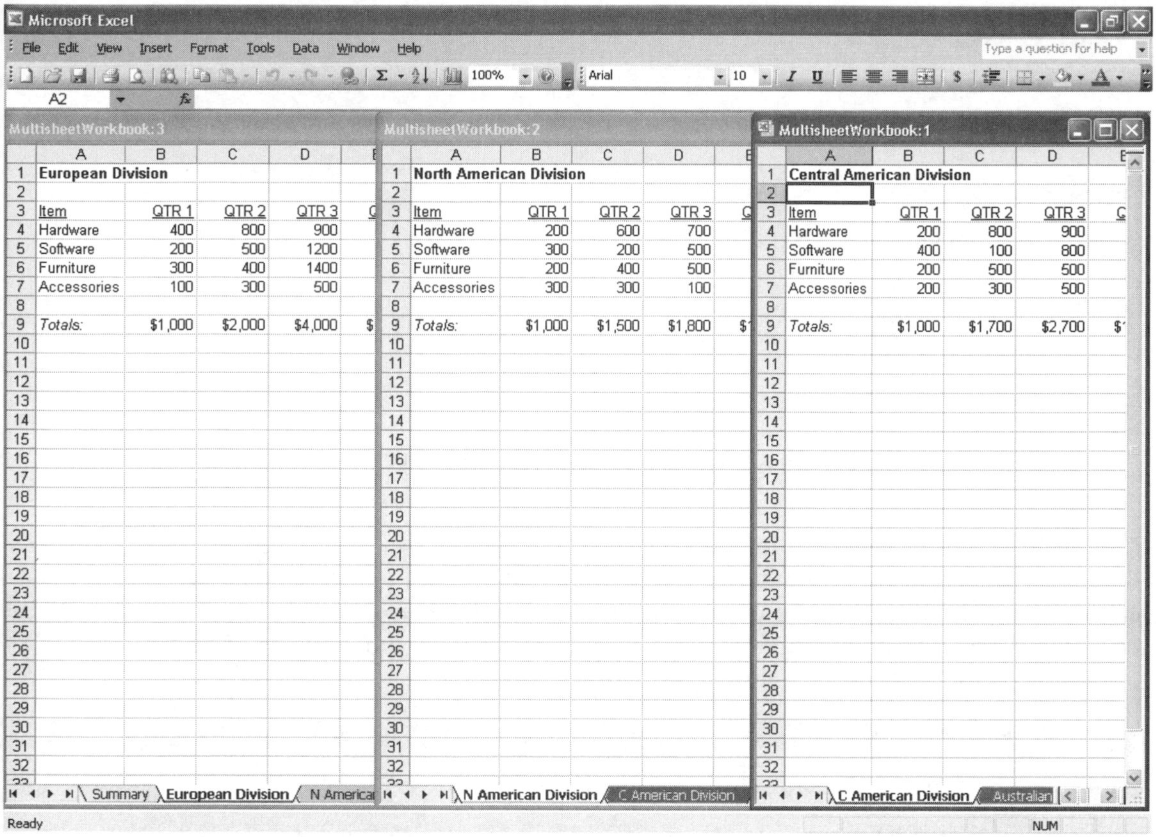

Figure 7-7: *A workbook with multiple worksheets arranged for easy viewing of data.*

Arranging worksheets allows you to view specific elements from multiple worksheets on-screen at the same time.

How to Arrange Worksheets

Procedure Reference: Arrange Worksheets

To arrange worksheets:

1. Choose Window→New Window to open the entire workbook in a new window.

2. Repeat step 1 until you have a new window for every worksheet you want to view in the workbook.

3. Choose Window→Arrange to open the Arrange Window dialog box.

4. Select the options you want.

5. Click OK.

ACTIVITY 7-2

Arranging Worksheets

Objective:

To arrange worksheets.

Data Files:

*   MultisheetWorkbook

Setup:

Close the file PrintPractice. Open the file MultisheetWorkbook.

Scenario:

You are working on the MultisheetWorkbook file and want to compare some of the values on the four named worksheets. To prevent having to click back and forth between worksheet tabs, you have decided to arrange the worksheets so you can view the contents of all four worksheets simultaneously, as shown in Figure 7-8.

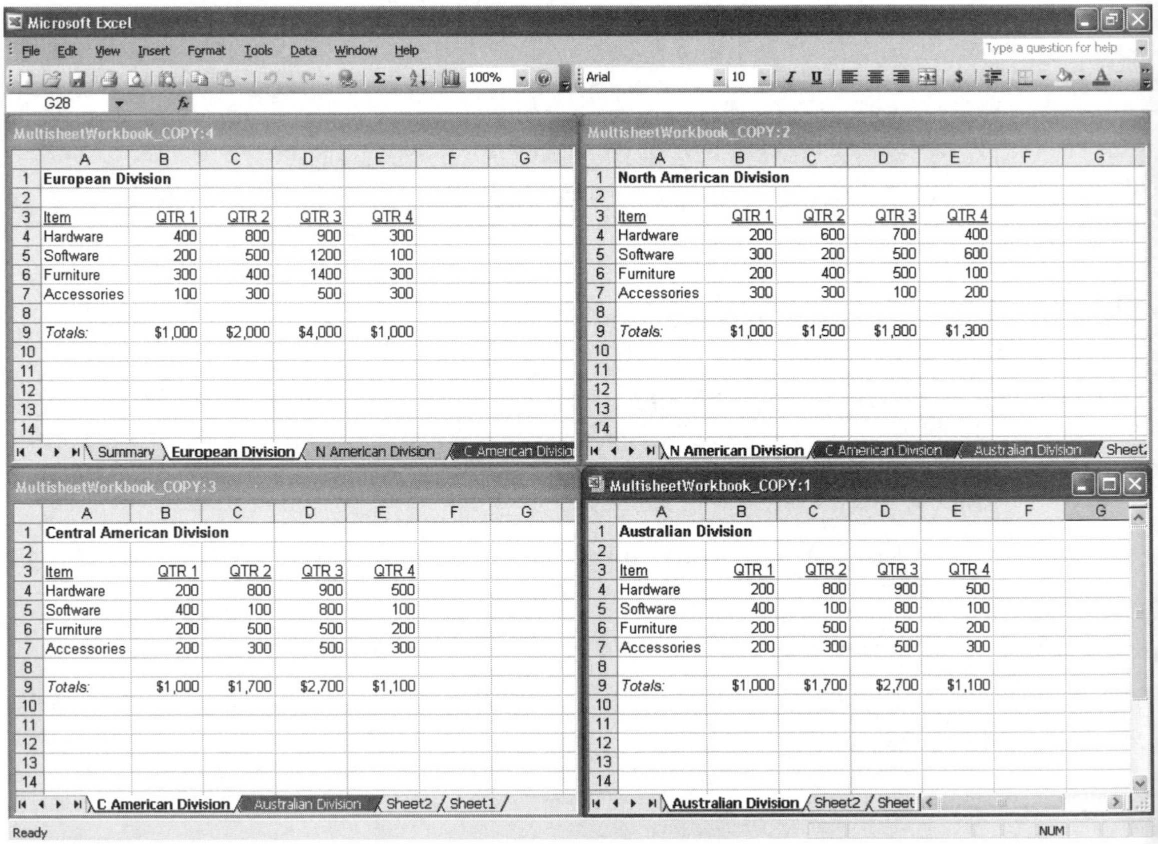

Figure 7-8: *Worksheets arranged for simultaneous viewing.*

What You Do	How You Do It
1. **Create three new windows.**	a. **Choose Window→New Window** to create the first new view of the entire workbook.
	b. **Choose Window→New Window** to create the second new view of the entire workbook.
	c. **Choose Window→New Window** to create the third new view of the entire workbook.
2. **Arrange the windows vertically.**	a. **Choose Window→Arrange** to open the Arrange Windows dialog box.
	b. **Select the Vertical option.**

c. **Check the Windows Of Active Workbook check box.**

d. **Click OK** to arrange the windows vertically.

3. **Arrange the windows horizontally.**

    a. **Choose Window→Arrange** to open the Arrange Windows dialog box.

    b. **Select the Horizontal option.**

    c. **Click OK** to arrange the windows horizontally.

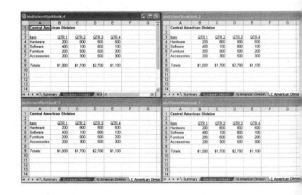

4. **Tile the windows.**

    a. **Choose Window→Arrange** to open the Arrange Windows dialog box.

    b. **Select the Tiled option.**

    c. **Click OK** to tile the windows.

5. **View each of the named worksheets in its own window.**

a. In the MultisheetWorkbook:1 window, **click the Australian Division tab** to view the Australian Division worksheet's contents.

b. In the MultisheetWorkbook:2 window, **click the N American Division tab** to view the N American Division worksheet's contents.

c. In the MultisheetWorkbook:3 window, **click the C American Division tab** to view the C American Division worksheet's contents.

d. In the MultisheetWorkbook:4 window, **click the European Division tab** to view the European Division worksheet's contents.

TOPIC C

Freeze and Unfreeze Rows and Columns

Another way you can customize a layout is to force a specific row or column to always appear on-screen. In this topic, you will freeze and unfreeze rows and columns.

The following figure, Figure 7-3, shows a worksheet that contains employee information.

	A	B	C	D	E	F	G	H
1				**Benjamin of Brussels**				
1				International Chocolate Distributors, Inc.				
2				U.S. Sales 2003				
3								
4	**Last Name**	**First Name**	**Region**	**Qtr 1**	**Qtr 2**	**Qtr 3**	**Qtr 4**	**Total**
5	Arman	Simon	East	$ 14,815.00	$ 13,100.00	$ 11,580.00	$ 17,300.00	$ 56,795.00
6	Bartholomew	Barbara	North	$ 24,500.00	$ 25,600.00	$ 22,000.00	$ 19,000.00	$ 91,100.00
7	Childs	Alice	West	$ 20,900.00	$ 22,600.00	$ 20,140.00	$ 24,400.00	$ 88,040.00
8	Greenburg	Linda	East	$ 15,900.00	$ 22,700.00	$ 17,600.00	$ 20,000.00	$ 76,200.00
9	Lundquist	Sam	North	$ 25,000.00	$ 34,000.00	$ 21,000.00	$ 35,000.00	$ 115,000.00
10	McTague	Michael	Northwest	$ 24,110.00	$ 54,812.00	$ 15,200.00	$ 25,600.00	$ 119,722.00
11	Quayle	Antonio	West	$ 25,600.00	$ 48,752.00	$ 30,300.00	$ 22,600.00	$ 127,252.00
12	Rivena	Orlando	South	$ 22,600.00	$ 58,445.00	$ 16,800.00	$ 22,700.00	$ 120,545.00
13	Stark	Oscar	Southwest	$ 22,700.00	$ 48,648.00	$ 36,855.00	$ 35,000.00	$ 143,203.00
14	Unger	Maria	Southwest	$ 23,300.00	$ 24,600.00	$ 21,380.00	$ 15,937.00	$ 85,217.00
15	Hanover	Caroline	East	$ 23,800.00	$ 27,700.00	$ 12,600.00	$ 35,000.00	$ 99,100.00
16	Jaen	Enrique	West	$ 54,826.00	$ 598,224.00	$ 24,100.00	$ 28,000.00	$ 705,150.00
17	Monder	Alana	Southwest	$ 31,200.00	$ 23,100.00	$ 17,700.00	$ 29,300.00	$ 101,300.00
18	Innoue	Chika	South	$ 50,224.00	$ 17,300.00	$ 15,200.00	$ 14,600.00	$ 97,324.00
19	Ryan	Maureen	Midwest	$ 15,500.00	$ 19,000.00	$ 30,300.00	$ 22,600.00	$ 87,400.00
20	Simmonds	Leon	West	$ 30,900.00	$ 24,400.00	$ 16,800.00	$ 24,513.00	$ 96,613.00
21	Clark	John	East	$ 14,815.00	$ 13,100.00	$ 11,580.00	$ 17,300.00	$ 56,795.00
22	Rapp	Amanda	North	$ 24,500.00	$ 25,600.00	$ 22,000.00	$ 19,000.00	$ 91,100.00
23	Booth	Cathy	Northwest	$ 20,900.00	$ 22,600.00	$ 20,140.00	$ 24,400.00	$ 88,040.00
24	Diehl	Jim	West	$ 15,900.00	$ 22,700.00	$ 17,600.00	$ 20,000.00	$ 76,200.00
25	Smith	Elizabeth	South	$ 25,000.00	$ 34,000.00	$ 21,000.00	$ 35,000.00	$ 115,000.00
26	Merkley	Katie	Southwest	$ 24,110.00	$ 54,812.00	$ 15,200.00	$ 25,600.00	$ 119,722.00
27	Cuzens	Beth	Southwest	$ 25,600.00	$ 48,752.00	$ 30,300.00	$ 22,600.00	$ 127,252.00
28	Saylor	Rachel	East	$ 22,600.00	$ 58,445.00	$ 16,800.00	$ 22,700.00	$ 120,545.00
29	Wilson	Tom	West	$ 22,700.00	$ 48,648.00	$ 36,855.00	$ 35,000.00	$ 143,203.00
30	Hartson	Sue	Southwest	$ 23,300.00	$ 24,600.00	$ 21,380.00	$ 15,937.00	$ 85,217.00
31	Sandler	Cheryl	South	$ 23,800.00	$ 27,700.00	$ 12,600.00	$ 35,000.00	$ 99,100.00

Figure 7-9: *A worksheet with a long vertical list and no frozen rows or columns.*

If you want to scroll down the list of names, it would make sense to have the heading row stay visible as you scroll, as shown in Figure 7-10.

Figure 7-10: *A worksheet with frozen columns and rows.*

Freezing and unfreezing rows and columns allows you to view specific elements of the worksheet on-screen at the same time.

How to Freeze and Unfreeze Rows and Columns

Procedure Reference: Freeze Rows and Columns

To freeze rows and columns:

1. Choose Window→Split to add split bars to the worksheet.

2. Position the worksheet contents and split bars where you would like them to freeze.

3. Choose Window→Freeze Panes to freeze the rows and columns.

Procedure Reference: Unfreeze Rows and Columns

To unfreeze rows and columns:

1. Choose Window→Unfreeze Panes to unfreeze the rows and columns.

ACTIVITY 7-3

Freezing and Unfreezing Rows and Columns

Objective:
To freeze and unfreeze rows and columns.

Data Files:

- PrintPractice

Setup:
Close the file MultisheetWorkbook. Open the file PrintPractice. If necessary, maximize the view of the PrintPractice file.

Scenario:
You are going to send the PrintPractice worksheet out for review. To make it easier for reviewers to identify the column headings, you've decided to freeze the Last Name column and the heading row.

At the last minute, before you send the file out for review, your manager calls and asks that you not freeze any rows and columns.

What You Do	How You Do It
1. Apply a split view to the worksheet.	a. **Select cell E15** to place the insertion point in the middle of the worksheet.
	b. **Choose Window→Split** to add the split lines to the view.

2. **Place the Last Name column heading in the first quadrant.**

   a. Using the top vertical scroll bar, **click the downward scroll arrow until row 4 appears at the top edge of the viewable region.**

   b. **Drag the horizontal split up** until only row 4 appears in quadrants 1 and 2.

   c. **Drag the vertical split to the left** until only column A appears in quadrants 1 and 3.

	A	E	F	G	H	I
4	Last Name	Qtr 2	Qtr 3	Qtr 4	Total	
15	Hanover	$ 27,700.00	$ 12,600.00	$ 35,000.00	$ 99,100.00	
16	Jaen	$ 598,224.00	$ 24,100.00	$ 28,000.00	$ 705,150.00	
17	Monder	$ 23,100.00	$ 17,700.00	$ 29,300.00	$ 101,300.00	
18	Innoue	$ 17,300.00	$ 15,200.00	$ 14,600.00	$ 97,324.00	
19	Ryan	$ 19,000.00	$ 30,300.00	$ 22,600.00	$ 87,400.00	
20	Simmonds	$ 24,400.00	$ 16,800.00	$ 24,513.00	$ 96,613.00	
21	Clark	$ 13,100.00	$ 11,580.00	$ 17,300.00	$ 56,795.00	
22	Rapp	$ 25,600.00	$ 22,000.00	$ 19,000.00	$ 91,100.00	

3. **Place the Qtr 4 and Total columns' values in the fourth quadrant, and then freeze the panes.**

   a. Using the right horizontal scroll bar, **click the right pointing scroll arrow until quadrant 2 contains only the Qtr 4 and Total columns.**

	A	G	H	I
4	Last Name	Qtr 4	Total	
15	Hanover	$ 35,000.00	$ 99,100.00	
16	Jaen	$ 28,000.00	$ 705,150.00	
17	Monder	$ 29,300.00	$ 101,300.00	
18	Innoue	$ 14,600.00	$ 97,324.00	
19	Ryan	$ 22,600.00	$ 87,400.00	

   b. **Click in cell K16** to deselect any selected cells.

   c. **Choose Window→Freeze Panes** to freeze the panes.

	A	G	H
4	Last Name	Qtr 4	Total
15	Hanover	$ 35,000.00	$ 99,100.00
16	Jaen	$ 28,000.00	$ 705,150.00
17	Monder	$ 29,300.00	$ 101,300.00
18	Innoue	$ 14,600.00	$ 97,324.00
19	Ryan	$ 22,600.00	$ 87,400.00
20	Simmonds	$ 24,513.00	$ 96,613.00
21	Clark	$ 17,300.00	$ 56,795.00

4. **Unfreeze the rows and columns, remove the split, and then save your work.**

   a. **Choose Window→Unfreeze Panes** to unfreeze the panes.

   b. **Choose Window→Remove Split** to remove the split.

   c. **Click the Save button.**

TOPIC D

Hide and Unhide Worksheets

You can also customize your layout by controlling when worksheets appear. In this topic, you will hide and unhide worksheets.

The following figure, Figure 7-11, shows a workbook with multiple worksheets.

	A	B	C	D	E	F	G	H	I	J	K	L
1	European Division											
2												
3	Item	QTR 1	QTR 2	QTR 3	QTR 4							
4	Hardware	400	800	900	300							
5	Software	200	500	1200	100							
6	Furniture	300	400	1400	300							
7	Accessories	100	300	500	300							
8												
9	Totals:	$1,000	$2,000	$4,000	$1,000							

Tabs: European Division / N American Division / C American Division / Russian Division / S American Division / Australian Division

Figure 7-11: *A workbook with multiple worksheets.*

Suppose you only want to work with the data on the first and last worksheets. By hiding (or unhiding, as needed) worksheets, you can arrange your workspace to accommodate your needs, as shown in Figure 7-12.

Lesson 7: Customizing Layout

	A	B	C	D	E	F
1	**Australian Division**					
2						
3	Item	QTR 1	QTR 2	QTR 3	QTR 4	
4	Hardware	200	800	900	500	
5	Software	400	100	800	100	
6	Furniture	200	500	500	200	
7	Accessories	200	300	500	300	
8						
9	*Totals:*	$1,000	$1,700	$2,700	$1,100	
10						
11						
12						
13						
14						
15						
16						
17						
18						
19						
20						
21						
22						
23						
24						
25						
26						
27						
28						
29						
30						
31						
32						
33						
34						
35						

H ◄ ► H \ European Division \ **Australian Division** /

Figure 7-12: *A workbook with multiple hidden worksheets.*

How to Hide and Unhide Worksheets

Procedure Reference: Hide Worksheets

To hide worksheets:

1. Select the sheet you want to hide.

2. Choose Format→Sheet→Hide.

Procedure Reference: Unhide Worksheets

To unhide worksheets:

1. Choose Format→Sheet→Unhide to open the Unhide dialog box.

2. From the Unhide Sheet box, select the worksheet you want to unhide.

3. Click OK.

ACTIVITY 7-4

Hiding and Unhiding Worksheets

Objective:

To hide and unhide worksheets.

Data Files:

- MultisheetWorkbook

Setup:

Close the file PrintPractice. Open the file MultisheetWorkbook. If necessary, maximize the view of the MultisheetWorkbook file.

Scenario:

You are going to send the MultisheetWorkbook workbook out for review. Your manager has asked that each division head only see the contents of the worksheet for their division. For example, when you send the workbook to the Australian Division manager, that manager should only be able to see the Australian Division worksheet. You have already prepared copies of the workbook for the European Division manager, the N American Division manager, and the Australian Division manager. You now need to prepare a copy for the C American Division manager.

At the last minute, before you send the file out for review, your manager calls and asks that you not hide Sheet2 for the C American Division manager.

What You Do	How You Do It
1. Hide the European, N American, and Australian Division worksheets.	a. Click the **Australian Division tab** to select the worksheet.
	b. Choose **Format→Sheet→Hide** to hide the worksheet.
	c. Click the **N American Division tab**, press and hold Shift, and then click the **European Division tab** to select both of these worksheets.
	d. Choose **Format→Sheet→Hide** to hide these worksheets.

2.	**Hide the Sheet1 and Sheet2 worksheets.**	a.	**Click the Sheet1 tab, press and hold Shift, and then click the Sheet2 tab** to select both of these worksheets.
		b.	**Choose Format→Sheet→Hide** to hide these worksheets.

\ Summary \ C American Division /

3.	**Save and close the workbook.**	a.	**Click the Save button.**
		b.	**Choose File→Close.**

4.	**Open the MultisheetWorkbook file, and then unhide the Sheet2 worksheet.**	a.	**Choose File→MultisheetWorkbook** to open the file.
		b.	**Choose Format→Sheet→Unhide** to open the Unhide dialog box.
		c.	From the Unhide Sheet list, **select Sheet2.**

Unhide

Unhide sheet:

European Division
N American Division
Australian Division
Sheet2
Sheet1

OK   Cancel

d. **Click OK** to restore Sheet2.

\ Summary \ C American Division \ Sheet2 /

Lesson 7 Follow-up

In this lesson, you customized the layout of the Excel application window. Customizing the application windows helps you work more efficiently while using Excel.

1. **What are some reasons you might want to customize the layout of your Excel work space?**

2. **This lesson introduced you to some basic methods for customizing how you interact with Excel. What other types of things would you like to customize in Excel and how might you find out if Excel supports those customizations?**

Follow-up

In this course, you used Excel to manage, edit, and print data. Storing data electronically is more efficient than storing it in a paper-based system because it allows you to quickly update existing data, run reports on the data, calculate totals, and chart, sort, and filter your data.

1. **What data are you currently working with that would be better stored in Excel? How might you begin the migration process from paper to electronic storage?**

2. **Consider your current work environment. What projects do you think would become more efficient if Excel was used either as an element of the project or if the entire project was controlled and manipulated within Excel?**

3. **Consider your current work environment. What data are you working with now that could benefit from being sorted, charted, or filtered to help make business decisions?**

What's Next?

The *Microsoft Excel 2003: Level 1* course helped you understand the basics of Excel and prepared you to go to the Element K course, *Microsoft Excel 2003: Level 2.*

APPENDIX A

Microsoft Office Specialist Program

Selected Element K courseware addresses Microsoft Office Specialist skills. The following tables indicate where Excel 2003 skills are covered. For example, 1-3 indicates the lesson and activity number applicable to that skill.

Core Skill Sets and Skills Being Measured	Excel 2003: Level 1	Excel 2003: Level 2	Excel 2003: Level 3
Enter and Edit Cell Content			
Entering, editing, and clearing text, numbers, and symbols in cells	1-4		
Filling series content using the fill handle tool	2-2		
Navigate to Specific Cell Content			
Finding and modifying or replacing cell content or formatting	2-5, 4-8		
Navigating to specific content (e.g., Go To)	2-5		
Locate, select, and insert supporting information			
Locating supporting information in local reference materials or on the Internet		1-9	
Using the Research tool to select and insert supporting text-based information		1-9	
Insert, Position, and Size Graphics			
Inserting, positioning, and sizing graphics		3-1, 3-2	
Filter Lists Using AutoFilter			
Filtering lists using AutoFilter		5-3, 5-4	

Core Skill Sets and Skills Being Measured	Excel 2003: Level 1	Excel 2003: Level 2	Excel 2003: Level 3
Sort Lists			
Sorting lists		5-1, 5-2	
Insert and Modify Formulas			
Creating and editing formulas	3-1		
Entering an range within a formula by dragging	3-1		
Using references (absolute and relative)	3-3, 3-4		
Use Statistical, Date and Time, Financial, and Logical Functions			
Creating formulas using the follow function categories: Statistical, Date and Time, Financial, and Logical (e.g., Sum, Min, Max, Date or Now, PMT, IF, Average)	3-2	4-3, 4-4, 4-5, 4-6, 4-9	
Create, Modify, and Position Diagrams and Charts Based On Worksheet Data			
Creating, modifying, and positioning diagrams and charts based on data contained in the active workbook		2-1, 2-2, 2-3, 2-4, 2-5	
Apply and Modify Cell Formats			
Formatting cells	4-1, 4-2, 4-3, 4-4, 4-5, 4-6, 4-7		
Applying AutoFormats to cells and cell ranges	4-9		
Apply and Modify Cell Styles			
Applying styles (e.g., applying a style from the Format→Style list)	4-10		
Modify Row and Column Formats			
Modifying height and width	4-3		
Inserting and deleting, hiding and unhiding rows and columns	2-4, 4-3, 4-4		
Modifying alignment	4-7, 4-Lab		
Format Worksheets			
Formatting tab color, sheet name, and background	4-2, 5-1		
Hiding and unhiding worksheets	7-4		
Insert, View, and Edit Comments			
Adding and editing comments attached to worksheet cells		1-4, 1-5, 1-6	
Create New Workbooks From Templates			
Creating a workbook from a template		1-1, 1-2	
Insert, Delete, and Move Cells			

Core Skill Sets and Skills Being Measured	Excel 2003: Level 1	Excel 2003: Level 2	Excel 2003: Level 3
Inserting and deleting selected cells	2-4		
Cutting, copying and pasting/ pasting special selected cells	2-1, 4-2		
Moving selected cells	2-1		
Create and Modify Hyperlinks			
Inserting and editing hyperlinks		1-7, 1-8	
Organize Worksheets			
Inserting worksheets into a work-book	5-3		
Deleting worksheets from a work-book	5-3		
Repositioning worksheets in a workbook	5-2		
Preview Data in Other Views			
Previewing print and Web pages	6-1, 6-2	5-Lab	
Previewing page breaks	6-5		
Customize Window Layout			
Splitting and arranging work-books	7-1, 7-2		
Splitting, freezing/unfreezing, arranging, and hiding/unhiding workbooks	7-1, 7-2, 7-3, 7-4		
Setup Pages for Printing			
Setting print areas	6-1, 6-6		
Modifying worksheet orientation	6-4		
Adding headers and footers to worksheets	6-2		
Viewing and modifying page breaks	6-5		
Setting Page Setup options for printing (e.g., margins, print area, rows/columns to repeat)	6-1, 6-3, 6-6		
Print Data			
Printing selections, worksheets, and workbooks	6-1, 6-3, 6-6		
Organize Workbooks Using File Folders			
Creating and using folders for workbook storage	1-5		
Renaming folders	1-5		
Save Data in Appropriate Formats for Different Uses			
Converting files to different file formats for transportability (e.g., .csv, .txt)		6-1, 6-2, 6-3, 6-4	

APPENDIX A

Core Skill Sets and Skills Being Measured	Excel 2003: Level 1	Excel 2003: Level 2	Excel 2003: Level 3
Saving selections, worksheets or workbooks as Web pages		6-4	

Expert Skill Sets and Skills Being Measured	Excel 2003: Level 1	Excel 2003: Level 2	Excel 2003: Level 3
Use Subtotals			
Adding subtotals to worksheet data		5-7	
Define and Apply Advanced Filters			
Creating and applying advanced filters		5-5	
Group and Outline Data			
Grouping and outlining data			3-6
Use Data Validation			
Adding data validation criteria to cells			1-5
Create and Modify List Ranges			
Creating and modifying list ranges		4-1, 5-Lab	
Add, Show, Close, Edit, Merge, and Summarize Scenarios			
Managing scenarios			4-2
Perform Data Analysis Using Automated Tools			
Projecting values using analysis tools (e.g., Analysis ToolPak)			4-7
Performing What-If analysis			4-3
Using the Solver add-in			4-4
Creat PivotTable and PivotChart reports			
Creating PivotTable reports and PivotChart reports			4-5, 4-6
Use Lookup and Reference Functions			
Using Lookup and Reference functions (e.g., HLOOKUP, VLOOKUP)		4-7, 4-8	
Use Database Functions			
Creating and editing Database functions (e.g., DSUM, DAVERAGE)		5-6, 5-Lab	
Trace Formula Precedents, Dependents and Errors			
Tracing formula precedents			3-1
Tracing formula dependents			3-2
Tracing formula errors			3-3
Locate Invalid Data and Formulas			

APPENDIX A

Expert Skill Sets and Skills Being Measured	Excel 2003: Level 1	Excel 2003: Level 2	Excel 2003: Level 3
Using Error Checking			3-4
Circling invalid data			3-4
Watch and Evaluate Formulas			
Using Evaluate formulas			3-5
Using cell Watch			3-5
Define, Modify, and Use Named Ranges			
Naming one or more cell ranges		4-1	
Using a named rage reference in a formula		4-2	
Structure Workbooks Using XML			
Adding, modifying, and deleting maps			7-1
Managing elements and attributes in XML workbooks (e.g., adding, modifying, deleting, cutting, copying)			7-3
Defining XML options (e.g., applying XML view options)			7-4
Create and Modify Custom Data Formats			
Creating and applying custom number formats	4-6		
Use Conditional Formatting			
Using conditional formatting			1-4
Format and Resize Graphics			
Using cropping and rotating tools		3-2	
Controlling image contrast and brightness		3-2	
Scaling and resizing graphics		3-2, 3-7	
Format Charts and Diagrams			
Applying formats to charts and diagrams (e.g., data series, plot area)		2-3, 2-4, 2-5	
Protect Cells, Worksheets, and Workbooks			
Adding protection to cells, worksheets, and workbooks			2-1, 2-2, 2-3
Apply Workbook Security Settings			
Using digital signatures to authenticate workbooks			2-10
Setting passwords			2-3
Setting macro settings			2-9
Share Workbooks			
Creating and modifying shared workbooks			2-4

APPENDIX A

Expert Skill Sets and Skills Being Measured	Excel 2003: Level 1	Excel 2003: Level 2	Excel 2003: Level 3
Merge Workbooks			
Merging multiple versions of the same workbook			2-8
Track, Accept, and Reject Changes to Workbooks			
Tracking changes			2-5, 2-6
Accepting and rejecting changes			2-7
Import Data to Excel			
Bringing information into Excel from external sources		6-6, 6-7	
Linking to Web page data		6-7	
Export Data from Excel			
Exporting structured data from Excel		6-1, 6-2, 6-3, 6-4	7-2
Publish and Edit Web Worksheets and Workbooks			
Publishing Web Based Worksheets		6-5	
Create and Edit Templates			
Creating a workbook template		1-3	
Creating a new workbook based upon a user-defined template			2-10
Editing a workbook template		1-1, 1-4, 1-5, 1-6, 1-7, 1-8, 1-9	
Consolidate Data			
Consolidating data from two or more worksheets			5-2
Define and Modify Workbook Properties			
Managing workbook properties (e.g., summary data)			1-4
Customize Toolbars and Menus			
Adding and removing buttons from toolbars			1-3
Adding custom menus			1-3
Create, Edit, and Run Macros			
Creating macros			1-1
Editing macros using the Visual Basic Editor			1-2
Running macros			1-1, 1-2
Modify Excel Default Settings			
Modifying default font settings			1-7
Setting the default number of worksheets			1-7
Changing the default file location for templates			1-7

LESSON LABS

Due to classroom setup constraints, some labs cannot be keyed in sequence immediately following their associated lesson. Your instructor will tell you whether your labs can be practiced immediately following the lesson or whether they require separate setup from the main lesson content.

LESSON 1 LAB 1

Creating a Basic Worksheet

Objective:

To create a basic worksheet.

Scenario:

Your manager has provided you with the following printed document, as shown in Figure 1-A.

Name				
Jane Seeger	500.25	0.00	108.13	254.90
John Wegman	108.13	504.28	157.90	108.13
Brenda Hall	342.78	56.23	22.78	79.34
Phil Smith	0.00	23.65	88.34	267.45
Bob Mallen	45.75	127.44	156.99	187.22

Figure 1-A: *A paper-based spreadsheet.*

She would like the paper document converted to an Excel spreadsheet.

You are somewhat familiar with Excel, and you have found that it would be easier for you if, when you press the Enter key, the insertion point moves one cell to the right (like the Tab key), instead of one cell down.

1. **Start Excel.**

2. **Create a new worksheet.**

3. **Enter the data from the paper-based worksheet into the new Excel file.**

4. **Open the Help system, and then locate and read the Help file that explains how to change which cell is selected after pressing Enter.**

5. **Make the changes necessary to force Excel to move to the next cell to the right after pressing Enter.**

6. **Save and close the file.**

When you are finished, you can compare your work to the PaperFile_SOLUTION file.

LESSON 2 LAB 1

Modifying a Worksheet

Objective:
To modify a worksheet.

Data Files:
- TierOneBaskets

Setup:
Close any files that might be open in Excel. Open the TierOneBaskets file.

Scenario:
Management has provided you with an Excel file named TierOneBaskets, as shown in Figure 2-A.

	A	B	C	D	E	F	G	H	I	J	K	L	M
1	Gourmet Gifts To Go												
2		Tier 1 baskets -- protected sales											
3													
4					Jan	Total							
5	Sales estimates (# of baskets):				75								
6													
7		Tier	Price										
8	Specialty	1	$28										
9	Cheese	1	$22										
10													
11													
12	Total value at selling prices:												
13				60.0%									
14	Our cost (% of price):												
15													
16	Overhead (% of seling prices):			25.0%									
17													
18	Net income poential :												
19													
20													
21													
22													
23													
24													
25													

Figure 2-A: *The existing copy of TierOneBaskets.*

Management has also provided you with a printout of what they would like the TierOneBaskets file to look like, as shown in Figure 2-B.

	A	B	C	D	E	F	G	H	I	J	K	L	M
1	Gourmet Gifts To Go												
2			Tier 1 baskets -- projected sales										
3													
4					Jan	Feb	Mar	Apr	May	Jun	Total		
5	Sales estimates (# of baskets):				75	100	85	150	175	210			
6													
7		Tier	Price										
8	Specialty coffee	1	$28										
9	Cheese	1	$22										
10	Fruit	1	$27										
11	Chocolate	1	$32										
12													
13													
14	Total value at selling prices:												
15													
16	Our cost (% of price):			60.0%									
17													
18	Overhead (% of selling prices):			25.0%									
19													
20	Net income potential :												
21													
22													
23													
24													
25													

Figure 2-B: *What TierOneBaskets needs to look like.*

You now need to modify TierOneBaskets so that it meets management's needs.

If you notice a slight difference between the fonts shown here and the fonts in the actual file, don't worry. A difference in font will have no effect on the outcome of this lab; the layout and functionality of the file is what is important.

Lesson Labs

1. Move the value in cell D13 to cell D14.

2. Insert five columns between the existing column E and column F.

3. Fill cells F4 through J4 with the text *Feb, Mar, Apr, May,* and *Jun,* respectively.

4. Fill in the number of baskets for each month.
   - Feb = 100
   - Mar = 85
   - Apr = 150
   - May = 175
   - Jun = 210

5. Below the existing row 10, **insert 2 rows.**

6. In cell A10, **type** *Fruit,* and then in cell A11, **type** *Chocolate.*

7. **Copy the value in cell B9 to cells B10 and B11.**

8. In cell C10, **type** *27,* and then in cell C11, **type** *32.*

9. **Edit cell A8 so that it reads** *Specialty coffee.*

10. Insert one cell between the existing cells C20 and D20.

11. Find the word *protected* and replace it with the word *projected.*

12. **Format the worksheet as needed.**

13. **Spell check the worksheet, correct any misspelled words, and then save your work.**

14. **Close the file.**

   When you are finished, you can compare your work to the TierOneBaskets_SOLUTION file.

LESSON 3 LAB 1

Performing Calculations

Objective:

To perform calculations on a worksheet.

Data Files:

- TierOneCalculations

Setup:

Close any files that might be open in Excel. Open the TierOneCalculations file.

Scenario:

Management has provided you with a financial worksheet, as shown in Figure 3-A.

	A	B	C	D	E	F	
1							
2				Tax Rate:	30%		
3	**Income**						
4	Specialty coffee baskets	$2,560.00					
5	Cheese baskets	$1,342.00					
6	Fruit baskets	$3,795.00					
7	Assortment baskets	$6,790.00					
8	Total Income						
9							
10	Expenses	$5,035.00					
11							
12	Net Income						
13							
14	Tax						
15							
16	Profit After Tax						
17							
18							

Figure 3-A: *The TierOneCalculations worksheet.*

You have been asked to calculate the Total Income, Net Income, Taxes, and Profit After Tax.

1. In cell B8, **use a function to calculate the Total Income.**

2. In cell B12, **write a basic formula that calculates the Net Income.** This is the amount derived from subtracting the Expenses from the Total Income.

3. In cell B14, **write a formula or function that uses an absolute reference to calculate the Taxes.** This is the amount derived from multiplying the Net Income by the Tax Rate.

4. In cell B16, **copy a formula or function that helps you calculate the Profit After Tax.** This is the amount derived from subtracting the Tax value from the Net Income value.

5. **Save and close the file.**

> When you are finished, you can compare your work to the TierOneCalculations_SOLUTION file.

LESSON 4 LAB 1

Formatting a Worksheet

Objective:

To format a worksheet.

Data Files:

*   TierOneFormatting

Setup:

Close any files that might be open in Excel. Open the TierOneFormatting file.

Scenario:

Management has provided you with an Excel file named TierOneFormatting, as shown in Figure 4-A.

	A	B	C	D	E	F	G	H	I	J	K	L
1	Gourmet Gifts To Go											
2	Tier 1 baskets -- projected sales											
3												
4					Ja	Fe	Ma	Apr	May	Jun	Total	
5			Sales e		#	#	#	##	175		210	
6												
7		Tie	Price									
8	Specialt	1	28									
9	Cheese	1	22									
10	Fruit	1	27									
11	Chocolat	1	32									
12												
13												
14			Total value at selling prices:									
15												
16			Our	1								
17												
18			Over	0								
19												
20			Net income potential :									
21												
22												
23												

Figure 4-A: *The TierOneFormatting file.*

Your management team has signed off on a mock-up of the TierOneFormatting, and they would like you to format the file so that it looks like the mock-up, as shown in Figure 4-B.

	A	B	C	D	E	F	G	H	I	J	K	L
1	Gourmet Gifts To Go											
2					Tier 1 baskets -- projected sales							
3												
4					Jan	Feb	Mar	Apr	May	Jun	Total	
5	Sales estimates (# of baskets):				75	100	85	150	175	210		
6												
7		Tier	Price									
8	Specialty coffee	1	$28									
9	Cheese	1	$22									
10	Fruit	1	$27									
11	Chocolate	1	$32									
12												
13												
14	Total value at selling prices:											
15												
16	Our cost (% of price):			60.0%								
17												
18	Overhead (% of selling prices):			25.0%								
19												
20	Net income potential :											
21												
22												

Figure 4-B: *What the TierOneFormatting file needs to look like.*

1. Adjust the height of any row that is either too tall or too short.

2. Adjust the width of any column that is either too narrow or too wide.

3. Move the contents of any cells that need to be moved.

4. Right-align the contents of column A.

5. Align the contents of any cells that do not have a consistent alignment with their neighboring cells.

6. Apply any necessary number formats.

7. Change the font type for the entire worksheet, and then change the size of the font for the title of the worksheet.

8. Apply bold formatting as needed.

9. Add borders and colors to cells to help delineate between different values in the worksheet.

10. Merge and center the cells as necessary.

When you are finished, you can compare your work to the TierOneFormatting_SOLUTION file.

Lesson 5 Lab 1

Developing a Workbook

Objective:

To develop a workbook.

Data Files:

- Harris

Setup:

Close any files that might be open in Excel. Open the Harris file.

Scenario:

A colleague has asked you to organize an Excel file named Harris. The file contains six worksheets. Your colleague would like you to name and color each worksheet tab, delete any unnecessary worksheets, order the worksheets in a way that makes sense, and then make a copy of the workbook.

1. Study each worksheet and then rename each worksheet tab with an appropriate name.

2. Add a unique color to each worksheet tab.

3. Reposition the worksheets in a logical order.

4. Delete any unnecessary worksheets.

5. Copy the entire workbook.

🖈 When you are finished, you can compare your work to the Harris_SOLUTION file.

LESSON 6 LAB 1

Printing a Workbook

Objective:
To print a workbook.

Data Files:
• LonePine

Setup:
Close any files that might be open in Excel. Open the LonePine file.

Scenario:
You are preparing an Excel file named LonePine for hard-copy distribution at a meeting. You would like the following:

• Each page of the printed copy to display the first five rows of the worksheet.

• The printout to appear in Landscape format.

• "Page X of Y" to appear at the bottom of every printed page (X equals the current page being viewed and Y equals the total number of pages in the printed document).

• A hard page break where a new month starts.

1. Set rows 1 through 5 as the print title.

2. Change the page orientation to Landscape.

3. Add a footer that identifies the current page and the total pages of the printed document (Page X of Y).

4. **Study the worksheet and add a page break between the last date in July and the first date in August and another page break between the last day in August and the first day in September.**

5. **Save and close your work.**

    When you are finished, you can compare your work to the LonePine_SOLUTION file.

LESSON 7 LAB 1

Customizing Layout

Objective:
To customize layout.

Data Files:
*   CompanyPayroll

Setup:
Close any files that might be open in Excel. Open the CompanyPayroll file.

Scenario:
You are working in the Excel file named CompanyPayroll. You want to split and freeze the rows and columns on the Payroll Info worksheet so that you can only see only the Last Name and Gross Pay column headings and their corresponding data. Additionally, you want to tile the view of the four worksheets in the workbook so that you can see the contents of each worksheet at the same time.

1. **Split the contents of the Payroll Info worksheet.**

2. **Drag the split bars so that you can see the Last column heading in the first quadrant and the Gross Pay heading in the second quadrant.**

3. **Freeze the rows and columns.**

4. **Create three new windows, and then make each worksheet visible in its own window.**

5. **Tile the worksheet windows.**

6. **Save and close the file.**

When you are finished, you can compare your work to the CompanyPayroll_SOLUTION file. The solution file may not open in tiled view. For help with tiling the windows, see "Arranging Worksheets" in the Customizing Layout lesson.

NOTES

SOLUTIONS

Lesson 1

Activity 1-1

1. Each graphic on the left has a specific component of a spreadsheet highlighted by a thick black box. Match the highlighted component in the graphics with their corresponding names on the right.

Solutions

e

	A	B	C
1			
2			
3			
4			
5			
6			

a. Data

d

	A	B	C
1			
2			
3			
4			
5			

b. Range

c

D16

	A	B	C
1			
2			
3			
4			
5			
6			
7			
8			

Sheet1 / Sh

c. Column

b

	A	B	C
1			
2			
3			
4			
5			
6			
7			
8			

d. Row

a

	A	B	C
1			
2			
3		$372.67	
4			
5			
6			

e. Cell

2. Each graphic on the left has a specific component of the Excel environment highlighted by a thick black box. Match the highlighted component in the graphics with their corresponding names on the right.

_c_   a.   Tab scrolling buttons

_i_   b.   Formatting toolbar

_e_   c.   Name Box

_j_   d.   Formula Bar

_h_   e.   Title bar

_a_   f.   Standard toolbar

_f_   g.   Task pane

_b_   h.   Worksheet tabs

_g_   i.   Active cell

_d_   j.   Menu bar

Activity 2-2

4. **Which are good candidates for AutoFill?**

   ✓ a) Adding Q1 through Q4 as headings for fiscal quarters.

   ✓ b) Adding the days of the week.

   c) Adding employee sales totals.

   ✓ d) Adding the consecutive years 1990 through 2003.

Activity 2-3

4. **Consider the following: Your manager asks you to clear a range of data in a worksheet. You do so, but then a short while later your manager returns to say he has made a mistake. He actually wants to keep the data you just deleted. Which action would most quickly return the deleted data to the worksheet?**

   ✓ a) Undo

   b) Clear

   c) Redo

   d) Edit

Lesson 3

Activity 3-1

2. **What is the January total?**

   a) 766.76

   ✓ b) 741.49

   c) 762.58

   d) 901.53

GLOSSARY

absolute reference
A cell reference in a formula that does not change when you copy the formula.

active cell
The cell that is selected when Excel creates a new worksheet.

application window
Usually fills the entire screen and provides an interface for you to interact with Excel. This is Excel's outer window.

argument
Data enclosed in parentheses (included in functions).

cell
The intersection of a column and a row.

cell reference area
Displays the name of the current or active cell.

column
A boundary within a worksheet that extends vertically through all the rows and holds data.

fill handle
The box at the corner of a cell or range that you can use to activate the Excel AutoFill feature. When a cell or range of cells contains data that you can display in increments, drag the fill handle to the left, right, up, or down to fill a range with data.

font
A set of characters that share several common qualities.

footer
Text that prints at the bottom of each page.

formula
A set of instructions that you enter in a cell to perform calculations.

formula bar
Displays the contents of the active cell in a workbook.

function
A built-in formula.

header
Text that prints at the top of each page.

order of operations
A sequence of computations that a formula follows to arrive at a desired result.

print title
A cell or range of cells selected to repeat at the top edge or left edge of a printed copy of a worksheet, respectively.

relative reference
A cell reference that is automatically updated by Excel whenever a formula or function is copied from an originating cell to a destination cell.

row
A boundary within a worksheet that extends horizontally through all of the columns and holds data.

sheet tabs
Used to navigate between worksheets in a workbook.

status bar
Displays information about a selected command and Excel's current state.

GLOSSARY

style
A collection of individual format options that you can apply at the same time to selected cells.

tab scrolling buttons
Used to scroll the display of worksheet tabs one at a time or display the first or last grouping of sheet tabs within a workbook.

title bar
Located across the top of the application window, the title bar displays the name of the application and the active workbook.

toolbar
Buttons that provide quick access to Excel's most frequently used commands.

workbook window
Appears within the application window and displays a workbook in which to enter and store data. This is Excel's inner window.

INDEX

INDEX

M

margins, 170
  setting, 170

N

navigating techniques
  using the keyboard, 8
  using the mouse, 8
number formats, 111
  applying, 112
  creating custom, 115

O

order of operations, 62

P

page breaks, 178
  inserting, 178
  removing, 179
page orientation, 173
Paste Special command, 95
print titles, 158
  setting, 160
printing a range, 180

R

Redo feature, 39
relative reference, 77
rows, 5
  changing height, 102

S

selecting data, 12
series of data
  filling cells, 35
sheet tabs, 5
spell checking, 56
spreadsheet
  definition of, 3
status bar, 5
styles, 129
  applying, 130

T

tab scrolling buttons, 5
tabs, 137
  formatting, 137
title bar, 5
toolbars, 5

U

Undo feature, 39
Unhide command, 103

W

workbook window, 3
workbooks, 3, 4, 5
  copying, 150
  saving, 19
  tabs, 137
worksheets, 3, 4, 5
  arranging, 193
  copying, 147
  pasting
  hiding, 202
  inserting, 144
  deleting
  modifying, 30
  modifying data, 129
  navigating cells, 8
  repositioning, 142
  spell checking, 56
  splitting, 189
  unhiding, 202

Your notes: _____

_____

_____

_____

_____

_____

_____

_____

_____

_____

_____

Your notes: _____

_____

_____

_____

_____

_____

_____

_____

_____

_____

_____